## CONTENTS

## CONTENTS - FIGURES AND TABLES

# EXECUTIVE SUMMARY

This report aims to: <u>a</u>) provide an understanding of methods for estimating the size of drug using populations in Scotland, <u>b</u>) discuss issues involved in interpreting prevalence information and <u>c</u>) outline options for future prevalence research.

**Section 1.** How useful is prevalence estimation? Do policy makers and service providers require prevalence estimates or are other indicators of drug misuse sufficient? Is public expenditure on combating drug misuse justified by the actual level of drug misuse? Discussion of these issues provides a framework for considering various forms of prevalence estimation. Can prevalence, of illegal and illicit activities, be determined by asking people about their drug use or is it necessary to construct a model of the 'hidden' population? Would a National Drug Survey provide all necessary prevalence information? Hypothetical examples from the fields of education, prevention and treatment highlight the various types of prevalence data required to address specific issues.

**Section 2.** Prevalence estimation requires detailed consideration of empirical, scientific and policy issues and realistic expectations as to what studies can achieve. In view of the extensive literature on conducting prevalence studies and technical issues regarding estimates, this report critically reviews a range of methods which could be used in Scotland. Three types of direct method - enumeration, needs assessment and surveys are assessed with illustrative examples. The limitations of direct prevalence estimation have led to the development of indirect methods in which information on known drug use and users is used to estimate the extent of the hidden population. Four indirect methods are appraised: capture-recapture, multiplier techniques, network analysis and synthetic estimation. The section concludes with a brief discussion of other forms of prevalence estimation such as hair/urine analysis and system dynamic models.

**Section 3** provides guidance on selecting an appropriate method for different objectives (e.g. local, national, recreational/problem drugs). Method selection should be a joint decision between purchasers and providers. It is not feasible to recommend prevalence estimation techniques solely on scientific criteria.

**Section 4** presents a digest of views on prevalence estimation from Scottish Health Boards. There is considerable variation both in available information and planned activities relating to drug misuse. Existing surveillance and research is not generally thought to be satisfactory. There is a widely held view that a National Survey would be useful as a supplement to improved local surveillance.

Given the widespread belief that drug misuse will continue to increase throughout Scotland, **Section 5** outlines options for enhancing routine data collection, evaluating drug policies and co-ordinating local and national surveillance and research. Finally, the option of a National Survey, which could provide a focus for Scottish drug prevalence estimation, is re-evaluated.

# 1. INTRODUCTION

There is growing concern that drug misuse is increasing in Scotland and more generally throughout the world. In the former Soviet Union, for example, the social and economic changes which have occurred since the mid-1980s are reported to have been accompanied by rapid growth in drug abuse[1]. Within Europe there is vigorous debate about which policies have the greatest impact on the drug problem. Prevalence estimates are often cited as evidence that a certain policy in a certain country is more successful because of lower prevalence estimates compared to other countries. However such comparisons are invariably flawed as the estimates are not derived from homogeneous methodologies[2].

The view that drug misuse is increasing in the UK is usually derived from survey data and certain indicators such as the number of 'addicts' in treatment, yet these data are open to multiple interpretation (see SECTION 2). In their recent report on <u>Psychosocial Disorders in Young People</u>[3] Michael Rutter and David Smith argue that:

> *if there has been such a marked rise over time (in drug misuse and other psychosocial disorders), then it ought to be possible to provide an equally dramatic fall if we understood the processes that underlined the rise.*

While this report is not directly concerned with the causes of drug use, it nevertheless aims to inform understanding of the prevalence data which underpin wider enquiry. On a more practical level, the recent Scottish Office <u>Drugs Task Force Report</u>[4] stresses that:

> *future service development must be based on a systematic and comprehensive assessment of the nature, extent and distribution of need.*

## 1.1. WHY ESTIMATE PREVALENCE OF DRUG MISUSE?

During the last decade there has been a massive increase in publicly funded responses to drug misuse in the UK. In 1993/94, the Scottish Affairs Committee[5] noted that the total cost to the public purse was £37.3 million, comprising £21.1 million for law enforcement, £6.5 million for prevention and education and £9.7 million for treatment and rehabilitation. Despite the many caveats surrounding these figures it is clear that there is substantial public expenditure on drug misuse, let alone the indirect effects on economic activity and use of medical resources. In 1988 the aggregate cost of drug misuse to society in the United States was estimated to be $58.3 *billion*[6].

With regard to the direct public costs, it is legitimate to ask whether taxpayers are receiving value for money. An investigation in 1992/3 by researchers at the Centre for Health Economics in York[7] lead to the conclusion that:

*the agencies of government spend hundreds of millions of pounds on a problem whose magnitude and trends are unknown....while asserting that the drug problem is "considerable" and their efforts to contain it "successful".*

Underlying this argument is the view that the Government does not measure the real extent of drug use, which the same authors suggest could be done 'simply and with moderate expenditure' by a national survey of drug use. In other words if a random and representative sample of the general population are asked about their drug use, their (true and accurate?) responses would enable government agencies to rationally allocate resources.

## 1.2. SHOULD THERE BE A NATIONAL SURVEY?

Several European countries as well as the United States do have regular surveys specifically concerning drug use, whereas in the UK questions on drug use are usually incorporated into surveys on other topics such as crime, sexual behaviour and education. Issues concerning drug surveys are discussed in more detail in SECTION 2.1.3. Suffice to say, there are a number of methodological and empirical issues, which cast doubt on the reliability and validity of survey data. One only has to think of the errors in surveys of political opinion to imagine the possible errors in surveys of socially disapproved and illegal activities - particularly where such activities involve a relatively small proportion of the population.

In view of the real or perceived problems of asking people directly about drug use, a number of indirect prevalence estimation techniques have been developed. These methods depend on collecting data from sources with information on known drug use or users and constructing a model to project from known to unknown or hidden populations. The modelling process, can range from simple extrapolation to complex multivariate analysis (see SECTION 2.2). While indirect methods have acquired an air of scientific credibility, it is often unclear whether the assumptions required by many models in order to validate indirect prevalence estimates are met.

## 1.3. PREVALENCE AND POLICY

With a few notable exceptions, most work on prevalence estimation has been conducted in the United States. The US National Institute of Drug Abuse (NIDA) conducts regular household surveys and supports a wide range of prevalence estimation studies[8]. However, in the US:

*most drug policy decisions...are now made without regard to what has been learned from prevalence estimation, partly because of policy-makers' perception of their limited credibility and partly because the policy process is weakly linked to prevalence estimates.[9]*

A further difficulty noted in discussing the UK situation is that:

*models (based on epidemiological data) that could be used for policy making are woefully imprecise.*[10]

Although the links between prevalence and policy are at present fairly tenuous, there are three main policy areas which could be influenced by drug misuse epidemiology: resource allocation, targeting sub-populations and evaluating interventions. It is important to identify the appropriate types of epidemiological information for different policy objectives and the resources required for conducting investigations and analysis (see FIGURE 1).

FIGURE 1. **Interaction between prevalence estimation and scientific, practical and policy issues.**

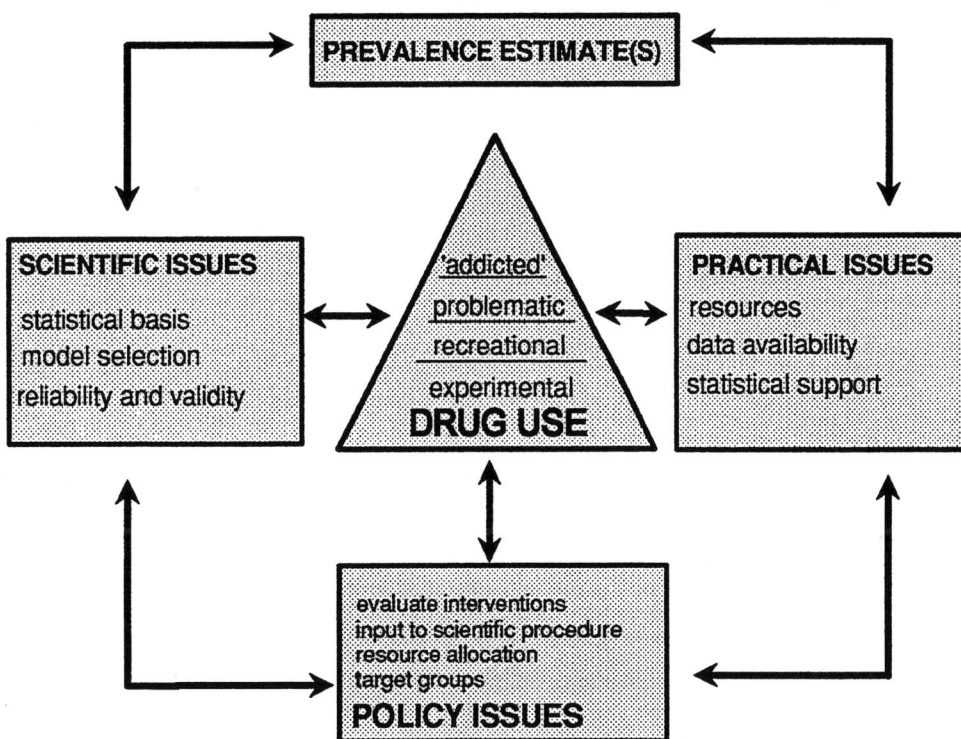

Consider, for instance, resource allocation to drug treatment programs. The most relevant information would be estimates of the number of people likely to participate in treatment. A general population survey is likely to be of little value for such a low prevalence form of behaviour (see SECTION 2.1.3). Even assuming that reliable data were available at a national level, would they be of any value without regional breakdowns? If there are regional differences are these associated with different forms of drug use, social conditions etc.? Probably the most efficient way of addressing this issue would be a series of local studies paying particular attention to case-definition and understanding the aetiology of drug use. Often such local studies begin with enumeration of known drug users (see SECTION 2.1.1) and/or a needs assessment (see SECTION 2.1.2). Both methods can be used, at a local level, to estimate the prevalence of hidden drug use.

Another policy recommended by the Advisory Committee on the Misuse of Drugs (ACMD)[11] is to 'discourage new recruitment into experimentation with drugs'. In this example, a rather different population is being addressed. Evaluation of this policy at a national level would require trend data over a number of years and surveys among young adults might be the appropriate methodology. As Britain does not have a regular survey on drug use it is necessary to rely on one-off drug surveys and surveys among young people (most of which are conducted by polling organisations). Determining prevalence of drug use among schoolchildren could also be an important means of addressing this issue but there are considerable methodological difficulties in conducting school surveys[12] (see SECTION 2.1.4).

While many drug related policies do require some assessment of absolute levels of drug use, there are other areas where trend data may be sufficient, particularly if factors influencing the trends can be identified. For example, an increase in medical emergencies involving ecstasy does not necessarily indicate a rise in the prevalence of ecstasy use but could be useful for formulating drug prevention policies. Unlike Spain[13], for example, Scotland has no recording system for drug-related medical emergencies (see OPTION 4, SECTION 5).

## 1.4. STRUCTURE AND SCOPE OF THIS REPORT

This reports has three main aims:

- **To provide a critical, yet accessible and practical, review of methods for estimating various forms of drug use in Scotland at national and local levels.**

- **To consider whether and how the information obtained from such studies can be linked to policies on treatment, prevention and other issues.**

- **To outline options for future prevalence estimation in Scotland and for achieving scientific and policy objectives.**

In SECTION 2, prevalence estimation techniques are reviewed with examples from Scotland, the rest of the UK and beyond. The main features of each technique are described together with limitations and assumptions. However this in not a complete manual for conducting studies. There are two reasons for this. First, there already is such a manual[14], produced by Richard Hartnoll and colleagues at the *Drug Indicators Project* (DIP) in London in 1985. The DIP manual focuses on how to conduct local studies and contains a wealth of detailed practical information and advice. The second reason is that, while the DIP manual does not provide much technical information on some methods, there is now a large body of specialist literature on statistical and technical issues surrounding prevalence estimation[15]. This information cannot be translated into a 'cook-book' and it is essential to consult source material.

This report conveys information regarding the reliability and validity of the various prevalence estimation techniques within the Scottish context. Type of drug (mis)use, geographical location and social setting and policy requirements are all factors which must be taken into consideration in choosing the appropriate technique. Data requirements, statistical skills, desired precision and available resources must also be heeded in conducting prevalence studies. SECTION 3 provides guidance on method selection.

After reviewing methods, SECTION 4 provides a digest of current prevalence activities in Scottish health board areas. This information was obtained from a short questionnaire sent to all Drug Action Team Chairpersons and Drug Misuse Co-ordinators in Scotland (see APPENDIX A). The questionnaire also sought views on what kinds of drug prevalence data should be sought, locally and nationally. Finally, SECTION 5 outlines options for enhancing routine data collection, evaluating drug policies and co-ordinating local and national surveillance to underpin the Government's recommendation that 'more effort should be put into producing reliable estimates of the extent of drug misuse in Scotland'[4]

# 2. TECHNIQUES FOR ESTIMATING DRUG USE PREVALENCE

A large number of substances are taken in Scotland by various routes (e.g. orally, intravenously, nasally) to achieve psychic effects. The 1994 Scottish Drugs Misuse Bulletin[16] reports 22 substances or combinations (excluding alcohol) taken by the 4,772 people reported to the Scottish Drugs Misuse Database by medical practitioners and treatment agencies in 1993/4. No single prevalence study is likely to cover the entire spectrum of drug use. In practice, prevalence studies focus on particular groups of users, such as opiate users or injectors which are of concern at a particular time in a specific location.

**TABLE 1. Four aspects of prevalence estimation.**

| locale | population | types of drug use | information required |
|---|---|---|---|
| national, local, urban, rural | total, young adults, school children, people in need of treatment/services | illicit use of prescribed drugs, illegal use of controlled drugs, experimental use 'problematic use' | prevalence, incidence, frequency of use, trends, user characteristics |

The issues highlighted in FIGURE 1 and TABLE 1 should be carefully considered when planning a prevalence study. Defining the combination of factors which underpin a particular study will help in choosing the most appropriate method or range of methods.

As noted in SECTION 1.4 this report is not a full manual, but rather aims to provide readers with an understanding of the key features of the various prevalence estimation methods. This section is divided into two sub-sections. SECTION 2.1 deals with methods where prevalence is determined by counting cases in the population of interest. SECTION 2.2 describes a range of methods which involve constructing a model of the total population of drug users based on samples of known drug users.

## 2.1. DIRECT METHODS

### 2.1.1. Enumeration of Known Users

This is the usual, and probably essential, starting point for any prevalence study concerned with 'problematic' drug use (however loosely defined) in a well defined geographical area (from a city downwards). The method consists of nothing more than counting (enumerating) the number of known drug users who meet a case definition from one or more sources, taking into account people who are counted more than once.

The simplest form of enumeration consists of collecting identifier information from all agencies in a given location who come into contact with users who meet a specified case definition. Parker and colleagues[17] identified 10 sources in the Wirral area of

7

Merseyside in 1984-85. Their case definition was simply <u>problem drug use</u> as evidenced by the involvement of official agencies.

In Glasgow, an attempt to enumerate known drug injecting during 1990 was more problematic because many agencies did not have information on injecting status and also their definitions of drug use were tailored to their own requirements. For example, police data on drug use consists primarily of information on people arrested under the Misuse of Drugs Act. There is no way of ascertaining whether such people are injectors, users or non-users. Other offences, e.g. those committed by drug users to finance the purchase of drugs, are not recorded as being drug related (see OPTION 4, SECTION 5).

Multi-source enumeration depends on obtaining the co-operation of as many agencies as possible but has limitations both with regard to known and hidden users. If additional or better quality information is required there are two possible approaches. The first is to accept the limitations of the method and use the data as a baseline for one of the indirect methods (see SECTION 2.2). Alternatively, problems encountered in retrospective enumeration can be avoided by setting up a prospective system for data collection. A prospective system has the advantage of ensuring standardised case definitions and reporting procedures. In practice this is likely to meet with resistance since agencies usually have good reasons for their already in place systems of data collection. One drawback of prospective schemes is ensuring that all participants apply the same criteria in recording contact information.

The key source for enumeration information on problematic drug use in Scotland is the <u>Scottish Drugs Misuse Database</u>[16] [SDMD]. The SDMD contains information from a wide range of medical and non-medical agencies dealing with drug users. The usefulness of such databases in estimating prevalence has been questioned by Sutton and Maynard who note that:

> *Regional drug misuse databases...reflect the uptake of treatment services and the effectiveness of enforcement activity. Even if monitoring techniques (across the UK) are standardised, the proportion of total users included (in the databases) will be unknown and will fluctuate. Identified users are likely to be unrepresentative of the general drug using population, therefore the size of the problem will be unknown, changes in trends and statistics will be impossible to interpret and policy makers will be presented with an atypical picture of drug users.*[7]

Whether these are fair criticisms depends on whether the UK databases were <u>primarily</u> designed to inform overall drug prevalence and/or allocate resources for dealing with drug abuse. In fact their <u>main</u> objective was to extend the scope of notifications beyond medical practitioners and it is recognised that the databases only record drug users who come into contact with doctors or other services. The databases have been found to be useful for local service providers who are able to meaningfully interpret trends in their region's data[18,19]. Clearly if the data were used at a national level, this local knowledge might not be available and there would be scope for misinterpretation.

Not all policies require data on the absolute level of drug misuse. Trend data can be useful for identifying new drug consumption patterns and formulating policy directed towards target populations. In addition, the databases could provide excellent information for indirect forms of prevalence estimation which may overcome some of the problems identified by Sutton and Maynard[7].

A little used variation of this method is <u>community enumeration</u> where known drug users attempt to seek out all other users in defined locations.[14]

## 2.1.2. Needs Assessment

This is not, strictly speaking, a prevalence estimation technique, nor are there fixed rules for conducting assessments. Needs assessment involves 'looking at a representative sample of the drug misusing population, to ascertain social and health care needs'[14]. As ascertainment of these needs is usually involved in quantifying the resources required to meet them, prevalence is bound to be, at least informally, specified during such a procedure. This view is endorsed in the <u>Scottish Office Ministerial Drugs Task Force Report</u> which recognised that, 'for effective policy development and service planning, needs assessments and prevalence estimates should be combined'[4].

Several needs assessments have been conducted in recent years by the Scottish Drugs Forum (SDF). Assessments usually take 3-6 months, during which time a field-worker will work with local people to identify needs and formulate appropriate responses.

In 1992, a needs assessment was conducted in East Lothian with the operational aim of providing statistical and qualitative data on problem drug use in order to 'facilitate the development of a local strategy to guide development and prioritisation of services'[20]. TABLE 2 shows the methods used during the assessment exercise:

**TABLE 2. Methods used in 1992 Needs Assessment in East Lothian.**

1. Collation of data from document sources.
2. Semi-structured interview and questionnaires to workers coming into contact with drug users (e.g. social workers, health visitors, general practitioners).
3. Survey of 100 people aged 13-18 attending youth clubs.
4. Survey of 47 problem drug users (snowball sample-see SECTION 2.2.4).

The final report contains a great deal of interesting information about 'problem drug use' in East Lothian. Due to the nature of the assessment, most of the information relates to known drug users. Method 1 was judged to be *of limited value.* The survey of young people (method 3) gave some idea of prevalence - there were indications of increasing experimentation with drugs towards the younger end of the age spectrum.

Overall, the needs assessment approach provides a general overview of local drug misuse, but does not really enumerate the extent of the known or hidden population. Nevertheless, the basic framework of the needs assessment technique could be adapted to various forms of prevalence estimation - although additional resources and time would be required. For example, if the collation of data sources included identifier information it would be possible to use enumeration (see SECTION 2.1.1) and various indirect methods (see SECTION 2.2).

### 2.1.3. Population Surveys

Prevalence estimates - particularly of 'hard' drug users - in countries with national surveys, are often <u>not</u> obtained by direct extrapolation from survey respondents to the general population. This is well illustrated by the 1990 German postal survey of drug use among people aged 12-39 in the former West Germany[2]. In this survey a representative sample of 31,363 people were drawn from the residents' register and sent a self-completion questionnaire. 19,208 (62%) participated in the survey after several follow-ups (by post and personal contact) of non-responders. Various prevalence estimates were made; for current purposes we will focus on two groups:

HARD-DRUG USERS: **those who had taken opiates, amphetamines or cocaine at least 20 times in the last 12 months**
INJECTORS: **hard drug users who had also injected**

With each additional follow up, the proportion of respondents who took large quantities of alcohol or cannabis remained stable, whereas the proportion of hard drug users increased. Detailed studies of non-responders in the USA[21] indicate that a proportion of non-responders *do not* differ from responders with respect to the use of cannabis or cocaine (<u>neutral non-responders</u>). However, some non-responders (18% in the American study) were *more* likely to be taking these drugs. This group is referred to as <u>critical non-responders</u>.

The 'true' prevalence is an additive function of the behaviour of three groups:
$R_1$ *(responders)* + $R_2$ *(neutral non responders)* + $R_3$ *(critical non-responders)*

Prevalence rates among responders ($P_1$) of 'hard' drug use and injectors were 0.18% and 0.04% respectively. These rates also apply to neutral non-responders ($P_2$). Prevalence among critical non-responder ($P_3$) may be calculated from the following formula:

$P_3 = P_{1,2} * \mathcal{X}$   where $\mathcal{X}$ is a multiplicative factor derived from information about non-respondents.

The number of drug users (N) is therefore given by the formula:

$$N = P_1 * R_1 + P_2 * R_2 + P_3 * R_3$$

Determining factor $\mathcal{X}$ is crucial to the prevalence estimation procedure. One way of estimating the magnitude of factor $\mathcal{X}$ is from mortality data. In 1991 there were 2,100 drug related deaths in West Germany which was assumed to represent a mortality rate of 2-3% per year. Application of the addict multiplier method (see SECTION 2.2.3) yielded an estimate of 70,000 - 105,000 injectors which in turn yields an estimate of factor $\mathcal{X}$=36 to $\mathcal{X}$=57 (see TABLE 3). For hard drug users, factor $\mathcal{X}$ was estimated to be between 23-36, giving a plausible range of 206,000-304,000 hard drug users in West Germany. The use of drug related death data to correct for under-reporting in a population survey is a new departure and further work is required to assess the validity of this approach.

**TABLE 3. Variation in the estimated number of drug users in Germany, 1990.**

|  | $\mathcal{X}$=1 | $\mathcal{X}$=23 | $\mathcal{X}$=36 | $\mathcal{X}$=57 |
|---|---|---|---|---|
| number of hard drug users | 42,000 | **206,000** | **304,000** | 461,000 |
| number of injectors | 10,000 | 47,000 | **70,000** | **105,000** |

Prevalence estimates, particularly towards the more 'problematic' end of the spectrum, are unlikely to be accurate if they are simply extrapolated from survey responses. More sophisticated approaches require some mechanism for incorporating data from non-responders, although the value of factor $\mathcal{X}$ is likely to vary considerably with time and location.

Although the UK does not have a regular national survey devoted to drug use, five major surveys since 1990 have included some questions on drug use (see TABLE 4).

**TABLE 4. UK population surveys on drug use, 1990-1994.**

| TITLE | YEAR OF SURVEY | GEOGRAPHICAL COVERAGE | SUBSTANCES |
|---|---|---|---|
| Nation Survey of Sexual Attitudes and Lifestyles [NSSAL] | 1990/1991 | Great Britain | Injecting Drug Use |
| Drug Use and Drug Prevention [DUDP] | 1992 | Glasgow, Nottingham, Bradford, London Borough of Lewisham | 18 Drug Groups |
| British Crime Survey [BCS] | 1992 | England and Wales | 14 Drugs |
| Scottish Crime Survey [SCS] | 1993 | Scotland | 14 Drugs |
| National Psychiatric Morbidity Survey [NPMS] | 1993/4 | Great Britain | Alcohol, Tobacco, Drugs |

The DUDP[22] is of particular interest as it is the first general population survey dealing specifically with drug use to be published in the UK. The final report contains a wealth of information on the habits and views of the general public in four areas. In Glasgow, 972 people aged 16 and over were successfully interviewed (response rate:71%) during 1992. A booster sample of 258 people aged 16-25 living in areas of social deprivation was also interviewed. (The response rate cannot be calculated for this group as these interviews were achieved though quota sampling).

11

**FIGURE 2. Drug use and drug prevention survey conducted in Glasgow, 1992: Use of controlled or unprescribed drugs.**

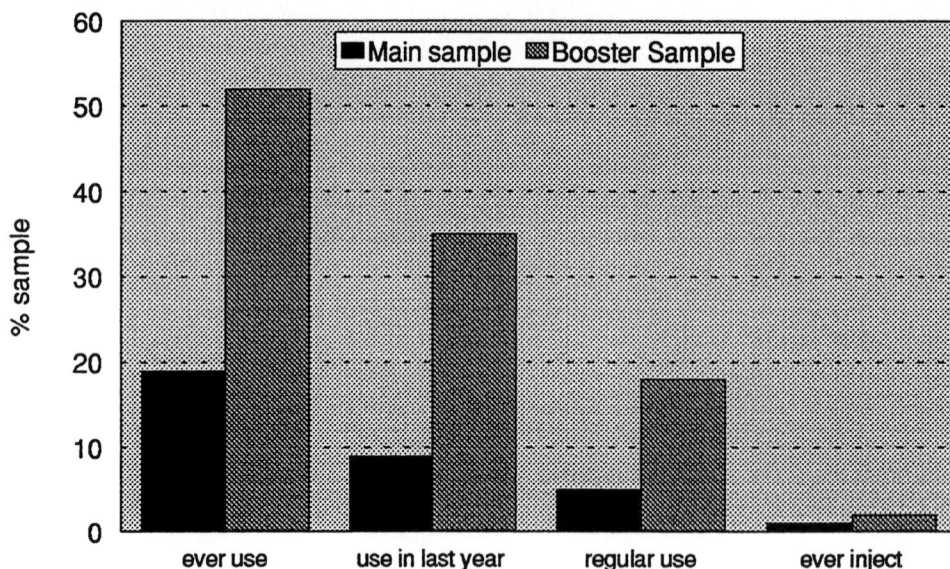

1. Proportions for 'regular use' and ever 'inject' are based on number of users in the last year.
2. 'Regular use' means at least once per month.
3. Main sample N=972, booster sample N=258 [ 16-25 year olds in areas of social deprivation].

FIGURE 2 shows that almost 20% of the main sample and over 50% of the booster sample had 'ever used' an illicit substance. Rates of reported injecting (which in 1990 was estimated using the capture-recapture method - see SECTION 2.2.1) were only 1% among regular drug users in the main sample and 2% in the booster sample. These percentages, extrapolated to Glasgow, suggest that the number of current injectors was about 2,000 in 1990, although this is based on self-reported injecting from only three individuals. If even one or two of these respondents ticked the box incorrectly or misunderstood the question, the estimate would be considerably different. Conversely, if one or two injectors did not report, for whatever reason that they had injected in the previous year, prevalence would be underestimated. Additionally, the estimate takes no account of critical non-responders - if the same correction factor was applied as in the German study discussed above the estimate would be about 14,000.

The prevalence of 'ever use' in the 1993 Scottish Crime Survey[23] (sample size 5,030 aged 16-59, response rate 77%) was 17%, very similar to the figure reported in the DUDP study in Glasgow. At this aggregate level of drug use, the impact of critical non-responders is probably minimal and therefore the prevalence of 'ever use' is probably within the confidence limits shown in FIGURE 3. A national survey also permits meaningful regional comparisons. Strathclyde and Tayside were similar to all-Scotland, Grampian and Lothian were significantly different from each other and Lothian was significantly higher than Scotland as a whole. As with the DUDP only a handful of people reported injecting drugs and prevalence estimates of this form of drug use are likely to be unreliable.

FIGURE 3. **Selected regional comparisons of drug use from the 1993 Scottish Crime Survey.**

Estimated prevalence of 'ever use' of controlled drugs among adults aged 16-59

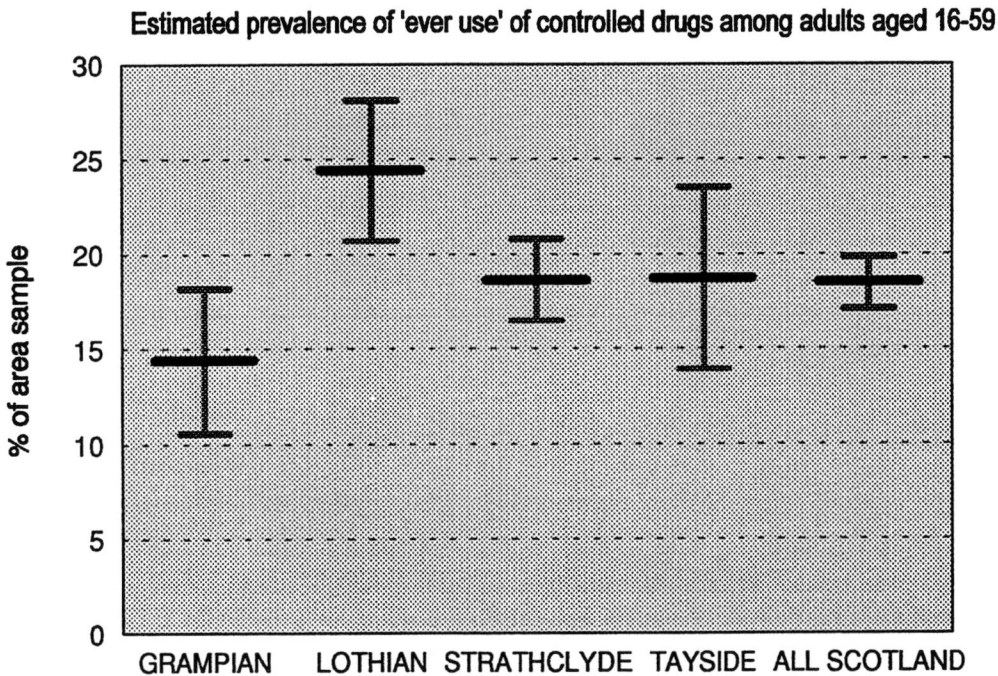

The major difficulty with population surveys concerns the interpretation and use of the data for policy purposes. Should the regional differences shown in FIGURE 3 be used, for example, in determining resource allocation for education and prevention? Factors which should be taken into account when considering the results from population surveys are shown in TABLE 5.

TABLE 5. **Limitations of population surveys on drug use.**

- Validity is difficult to assess. It is assumed that people can accurately recall past events and further, that they then truthfully report their behaviour.
- Responses may depend on respondent/interviewer characteristics and the way in which information is obtained. For example, a self-completion questionnaire within the context of a face to face interview on crime may suggest that researchers perceive drug use as bad. In self-completion questionnaires, some respondents may misunderstand the procedure or tick the wrong boxes by mistake.
- Very large samples are required for less common behaviour (e.g. injecting) and regional profiles.
- Sampling frames usually exclude non-households (e.g. homeless, prisons, hospitals).
- High non-response rates can be problematic.
- Large scale surveys are expensive to administer, conduct and analyse.

### 2.1.4. Surveys among People of School Age

The most recent data on drug use among people of school age in Scotland are contained in the 1993 Scottish Crime Survey. In this survey, people aged 12-15 who were resident in households where adults were interviewed were also asked to self-complete a questionnaire. This included a number of questions on knowledge of drugs and experience of drug use, which were similar although slightly more detailed than those in the adult questionnaire.

Four hundred and ninety five 12-15 year olds completed the questionnaire, although 8% did not answer the questions on drug use, compared to only 0.4% of adults. Hammersely[23] suggests two possible reasons for the high non-completion rate. First, young people who had never used drugs might have thought there was no need to answer drug related questions. Second, despite assurances on confidentiality, young people who had taken drugs concealed their usage by non-completion. These two factors, if operating, would pull 'true' prevalence rates in different directions, although in Hammersley's view the observed prevalence rates are probably underestimates.

The National Evaluation of Drug Education in Scotland[24] conducted four years earlier in 1989 reported much higher prevalence rates of drug use among people aged 12-15 than the SCS. This survey was conducted in classrooms with experienced drug researchers. Only 5 out of 1,197 pupils did not complete the section on drug use and the survey also contained checks for deception and exaggeration. While there are obviously advantages to this approach there is also the possibility that pupils who take drugs would not be in attendance when the survey was conducted.

Although school surveys have to contend with the problem of non-attendance, they are probably better than household surveys for eliciting information on drug use among young people. Many European countries conduct regular school surveys and recent analysis indicates that 'the use of cannabis by young people has been relatively stable or declining over the 1980s'[25]. In Amsterdam, for example, it has been suggested that the effective decriminalisation of possession of small quantities of cannabis has gradually stripped the drug of its glamour and has reduced its appeal to young people.

## 2.2. INDIRECT METHODS OF PREVALENCE ESTIMATION

Although population surveys have drawbacks with regard to characterising problematic drug use, other forms of direct enumeration can provide the starting point for indirect enumeration for populations of interest, e.g. injecting drug users. There are a number of indirect techniques, which generally require considerable fieldwork and/or statistical sophistication. It is therefore important to understand the assumptions on which the models are based and the limitations of resultant estimates.

### 2.2.1. Capture-Recapture

A large amount of discussion has been devoted to this method for two reasons. First, the capture-recapture method (CRM) is often, perhaps increasingly, perceived as having the greatest scientific credibility for estimating prevalence of injecting.

Second, CRM provides insight into the many factors which can affect prevalence estimation.

CRM refers to a technique developed over a century ago to estimate wild animal populations which involves 'capturing' a random sample who are then 'marked' and returned to their habitat. Subsequently, a second random sample are 'recaptured' and the number of marked animals from the first sample are observed. The ratio of marked animals to the recaptured sample size is assumed to be the same as the ratio of the first captured sample to the total population. Thus, if a 'capture' sample of 200 animals are marked and released and a 'recapture' sample of 100 contains 10 animals which are marked, the estimate for the total population would be 2,000 (i.e. 10:100=20:200). Begon[26] provides lucid justification for this method and an interesting overview of the many variants of CRM. Laporte regards CRM of such importance that it could 'bring about a paradigm shift in how counting is done in all the disciplines that assess human populations'.[27]

While the animal population estimates are based on sequential samples, in the case of human beings it is feasible (and often more practicable) to use simultaneous samples. Instead of identifying marks, identifier information is obtained from different sources which record contacts with the population of interest. Note that either sample may be labelled capture or recapture[*].

As an example of how this method can be applied to drug users, TABLE 6 shows a 'capture-recapture' matrix based on partial identifier information (gender, initials, date of birth, first part of post code) collected in Glasgow.

TABLE 6. **Number of individuals recorded in two lists of drug users in Glasgow, 1990.**

| treatment sample (capture) | HIV sample (recapture) present [N] | HIV sample (recapture) absent [N] | TOTAL |
|---|---|---|---|
| present [N] | 169 | 1107 | 1276 |
| absent [N] | 338 | unknown | |
| TOTAL | 507 | | |

The first sample consists of 1,276 individuals who received some form of treatment for drug use. The second sample consists of 507 people who had an HIV test and whose risk category was given as injecting drug use. Using the method described above the second sample contained 169 people who were also recorded in the first sample, so the total population estimate is 3,238. Confidence intervals for the number of unobserved drug users may be calculated using standard methods[28]. There are many variations of the basic capture recapture model which take account of factors such as inward and outward migration[29].

---

[*]An alternative terminology which may be more appropriate when using this method with human populations is contact-recontact (personal communication from Dr Michael Bloor). First because this is a more accurate description of the process of data collection and second because the term capture-recapture, while appropriate and accurate for animal studies, may reasonably be viewed as dehumanising when applied to people. However, it could also be argued that capture-recapture should be retained since introducing a new term for a well established method is likely to be confusing.

For this method to produce a reliable population estimate, certain criteria must be met:

- **All individuals have the same defining characteristics.**
- **Identification of individuals is accurate.**
- **Detection of an individual in a sample cannot change the individual's behaviour with respect to another sample.**
- **All individuals have the same probability of being sampled.**
- **Unobserved individuals behave in a similar way to observed individuals.**

In the example shown in TABLE 6, it is unlikely that any of these criteria are fully met, for the following reasons:

*Defining characteristics:* Treatment for drug use is heterogeneous ranging from one-off attendance at a drug project to in-patient psychiatric care. Injecting drug use (IDU) as a risk factor for an HIV test does not specify any time period (i.e. a person could have an HIV test with risk factor 'IDU', although they stopped injecting several years ago).

*Identification of individuals:* Errors can be made in recording identifier information or people can give false information.

*Individual behaviour:* If somebody has treatment for drug use they may be referred for an HIV test or might find out about testing facilities; thus people who received treatment for drug use may have been more likely to have received an HIV test than those who were not in treatment.

*Probability of being sampled:* If there are many drug users who, for whatever reason, never come into contact with treatment agencies or HIV testing, the estimate of the drug using population may well be wrong since it is entirely based on those who do.

Given these problems, there are two different approaches which might be taken:

The first, but less common, approach would be to design a prospective study. This would involve having a precise definition of drug users, protocols for data collection and monitoring of reporting agencies. Another variation of the prospective study would be to use one data source over a period of time. Although there are additional problems in relying on one data source, this approach has been used in the United States[30].

The second approach involves developing a more sophisticated model based on retrospective data. As already discussed, simple models are easy to use, they do not require much data and it is easy to understand the effect of violating assumptions (e.g. if the samples are not independent) - but they are likely to misrepresent the population and introduce bias into population estimates. On the other hand, sophisticated models can provide a better representation of the population but they require more data. Such models can require a considerable degree of statistical expertise and population estimates can be unstable (i.e. slight changes in the model can result in large fluctuations in estimates).

The data shown in TABLE 6 were part of a study to determine as accurately as possible the number of drug injectors in Glasgow in order to further determine the number of HIV positive injectors. In 1986, rates of HIV infection of up to 15 per cent were recorded among injectors in the north of the city who had a voluntary named HIV test[31] compared with a prevalence of almost zero 18 months previously. Thus HIV had become established into the drug injecting population which, although thought to be substantial, was at that time of unknown magnitude. It seemed possible that, given the high level of reported needle sharing among Glasgow injectors in 1987/88[32,33], HIV infection would spread rapidly both within and outwith this high risk group, as had occurred in Edinburgh between 1983 and 1985[34].

The prevalence study began with multi-enumeration. Identifier information was obtained from the sources shown in TABLE 7. Data collection varied from computerised records to manually searching through case reports. Many prevalence studies have ground to a halt at this early stage because agencies have refused to divulge or allow access to identifier information. Although very few agencies in Glasgow took this view, there is concern that European directives will make future access to named data very difficult[35].

**TABLE 7. Data sources used to estimate the prevalence of injecting drug use in Glasgow, 1990.**

| Data Source | | Number of Cases |
|---|---|---|
| 1. Scottish HIV test register | | 507 |
| 2. Drug treatment agencies | | 1 476 |
|    Non-residential community projects | 630 | |
|    Residential rehabilitation | 157 | |
|    Psychiatric hospital in-patients | 231 | |
|    General hospital in-patients | 194 | |
|    Addicts reported to the Home Office | 264 | |
| 3. Police [non cannabis drug offences] | | 508 |
| 4. Needle and syringe exchanges | | 1 179 |
| **Total number of cases reported** | | **3 670** |

As with the two sample example shown in TABLE 6 there are definition problems for all samples with the exception of needle and syringe exchange. Discussion with drug treatment agencies provided further information, e.g. about 90% of those seen at a certain agency were thought to be injectors. Other sources such as the Police are more problematic at this stage, although some checks can be made during analysis (see REFERENCE 36 for further details). Checking for false identifiers was not feasible. The likelihood that the HIV test register may be contaminated by false identifying information was considered, but the high level of overlap between this source and the treatment sample provided some assurance on this issue.

*Matching procedure:* Where there is incomplete identifier information (e.g. initials rather than full name), it is probably best to use a 'probabilistic' matching strategy whereby a computer program uses specified criteria to determine the probability of two cases being the same individual. The General Registrar Office, for example, uses probabilistic matching in linking the Scottish HIV Test and Mortality registers. In the Glasgow prevalence study, probabilistic matching based on gender, date of birth, initials and the first part of the post code was used to identify overlap cases. Clearly, matching on limited identification information may introduce error when identifying overlaps in two ways; 'false positives' could be recorded when two cases are thought to be the same individual while 'false negatives' could arise when overlaps are missed due to errors in recording identifier information. Careful checking of records at source and during the matching procedure was conducted to minimise these types of error. While the impact of errors in the present analysis is likely to be marginal, **it is impossible to rule out the possibility that errors in the four samples could result in a different model being selected** and consequently affect estimates of the number of unknown users (TABLE 9 below illustrates the process of model selection).

*Sample Interaction:* This term is used to describe a situation where detection of an individual in sample *A* alters the individual's behaviour with respect to sample *B*. For example if drug users arrested for drug offences then attend treatment agencies, the two samples will not be independent. In other words, drug users who are not arrested by the police may have a lower probability of being detected in the treatment sample than those who are. With only two samples there is insufficient information to detect interactions which could bias estimates. However it is important to examine the range of two-sample estimates (see TABLE 8). In this case the range is 3,828 to 8,642 and if the two extreme estimates are excluded the range reduces to 6,037 to 8,308. This relatively narrow range is not an inherent feature of the method - different sample sizes and overlaps could have resulted in widely discrepant two-sample estimates.

TABLE 8. **Estimates of the number of drug injectors in Glasgow, 1990 based on information from two samples.**

| SAMPLES | N1 | N2 | OVERLAP | TOTAL OBSERVED | ESTIMATED UNOBSERVED | TOTAL POPULATION | 95% CI |
|---|---|---|---|---|---|---|---|
| HIV & TR | 507 | 1,276 | 169 | 1,783 | 1,428-2,323 | 3,828 | 3,211-4,106 |
| HIV & NE-EX | 507 | 1,179 | 99 | 1,686 | 4,252-5,294 | 6,037 | 4,896-6,980 |
| NE-EX & TR | 1,179 | 1276 | 205 | 2,455 | 3,824-5,532 | 7,338 | 6,279-7,987 |
| NE-EX& POL | 1,179 | 508 | 75 | 1,687 | 4,576-7,871 | 7,985 | 6,263-9,588 |
| HIV & POLICE | 507 | 508 | 31 | 1,015 | 4,460-10,064 | 8,308 | 5,475-11,079 |
| TR & POL | 1,276 | 508 | 75 | 1,784 | 4,996-8,571 | 8,642 | 6,810-10,355 |

HIV=Scottish HIV Test Register, NE-EX= Needle and Syringe Exchange Scheme, TR=Treatment for Drug Use, POL=Non-Cannabis Drug Offences

Where three (or more) samples are available, it is possible to assess if there are any interactions between samples using a more sophisticated form of CRM. The three sample method does not require complicated statistics or computing[28]. With more than three samples, estimating population size requires the use of log-linear modelling. This is not a particularly complex procedure: Cormack[37,38] describes how to perform the analysis using the statistical computer program GLIM[39] and how to calculate confidence intervals. TABLE 10 gives key summary statistics for various models. Model 1, assuming independence between samples, does not fit the data well, judging from the $x^2$ statistic. Various combinations of sample interactions are then tested in order to see whether the model fit can be improved. The 'best' model, as judged from the $x^2$ statistic is model 3, with an estimate of 8,494 injectors.

**TABLE 9. Analyses of log-linear models used to estimate the number of injecting drug users in Glasgow, 1990.**

| Model | Type of Model | $x^2$ | D.F. | p value | u | N |
|---|---|---|---|---|---|---|
| 1 | All samples independent | 101.5 | 10 | 0.00 | 3 844 | 6 710 |
| 2A | Interaction between samples 1&2, 2&4 | 19.3 | 8 | 0.11 | 5 189 | 8 055 |
| 2B | Interaction between samples 1&2, 1&4 | 11.6 | 8 | 0.41 | 5 276 | 8 142 |
| 2C | Interaction between samples 1&2, 1&4, 2&4 | 6.8 | 7 | 0.56 | 6 000 | 8 866 |
| 3 | Interaction bt. samples 1&2, 1&4, 2&4, 1&2&4 | 2.9 | 6 | 0.83 | 5 628 | 8 494 |

*Samples: 1 = Scottish HIV-test register; 2 = Treatment agencies; 3 = Police; 4 = Needle and syringe exchange schemes. $u$ = Fitted value for missing cell (unknown injectors), $N$=total number of injectors.

Although the model has acceptable statistical properties (i.e. low $x^2$), it does not necessarily follow that the estimate for the number of unknown injectors is correct, since this estimate is based on the behaviour of known injectors. One way to verify the model is to repeat the analysis for stratified sections of the population and summate the results. If the sum of the stratified estimates is approximately the same as the unstratified estimate, it is reasonable to suppose that the latter is about right. If the stratified total is not similar this would indicate heterogeneity among sections of the population. TABLE 10 shows that in this case the stratified and unstratified estimates are very similar.

**TABLE 10. Estimated prevalence of drug injecting in Glasgow, 1990.**

| | N known Injectors | % known Injectors | Estimated no. of injectors | 95% Confidence interval | Population | Prevalence (%) |
|---|---|---|---|---|---|---|
| all cases | 2,866 | 34 | 8,494 | 7,491-9,721 | 628,000 | 1.2-1.5 |
| | | | | | | |
| males | 1,977 | 35 | 5,544 | 4,847-6,412 | 315 000 | 1.5-2.0 |
| females | 889 | 28 | 3,238 | 2,364-4,689 | 313 000 | 0.8-1.5 |
| male/female | | | 8,782 | | | |
| | | | | | | |
| age-group | | | | | | |
| 15-19 | 264 | 29 | 904 | 634-1384 | 88 000 | 0.7-1.6 |
| 20-24 | 1137 | 41 | 2750 | 2287-3317 | 104 000 | 2.2-3.2 |
| 25-29 | 878 | 33 | 2602 | 2043-3438 | 96 000 | 2.1-3.6 |
| 30-34 | 342 | 30 | 1138 | 792-1762 | 81 000 | 1.0-2.2 |
| 35+ | 245 | 16 | 1518 | 805-2595 | 259 000 | 0.3-1.0 |
| all age-groups | | | 8,912 | | | |

Although stratification provides a form of 'internal' validation, <u>external validation</u> requires some independent measures. One possible method for external validation is to compare the predicted and actual number of HIV positive injectors. The HIV prevalence rate among 503 injectors tested in a multi-site survey (in and out of treatment) was 1.4% (95% C.I. 0.4-2.5%). If there were 8,500 current injectors then there would be 119 HIV positive current injectors in Glasgow. Data to the end of December 1990[40] shows that there were 100 known HIV positive injectors from

Glasgow of whom 12 had died. As there are likely to have been several unknown HIV positive injectors (either to themselves or the register), the comparison provide some validation of the drug injecting prevalence estimate.

Another form of external validation could be provided by the 1992 Drug Use and Drug Prevention Survey (see SECTION 2.1.3). The 1992 DUDP estimate of 2,000 current injectors is obviously much lower than the 1990 CRM estimate of 7,500-9,700. Apart from the observation that prevalence could have declined between 1990 and 1992, there are many reasons for exercising caution in comparing the two estimates. The DUDP estimates are based on the positive reports of three individuals, whereas the CRM estimates are based on 2,866 known drug users. It is easy to adduce reasons which would lead one in the direction of supposing that the DUDP estimates are too low; conversely it could be argued that the CRM figure is too high. As both methods depend on a large number of assumptions, it is largely a matter of personal preference. The authors of the DUDP note that drugs professionals in Glasgow were more inclined to accept the higher estimate from the CRM study. However, this is a rather dubious form of validation since drug professionals might reasonably be expected to favour the higher estimate.

### 2.2.2. Multiplier Techniques

CRM studies usually involve extensive data collection and analysis. Another popular way of estimating prevalence which involves less work is to apply a multiplier to a cumulative number of events known to have occurred among a population of drug users. The best known and most frequently used multiplier is the annual mortality rate (sometimes called the lethality rate) for drug injectors which a number of studies have found to lie between 1-2%[41]. If it were possible to ascertain the number of deaths among drug injectors in a given location over a one year period, it might be reasonable to assume that the number of deaths are 1-2% of the active injecting population that year. There are two factors which need to be considered:

1. **The 1-2% rate nearly always stems from deaths among drug injectors attending treatment agencies. There is some evidence that the rate might be increasing due to the impact of HIV infection[42].**
2. **It is by no means easy to ascertain the number of drug related deaths (although the situation has recently improved in Scotland with the introduction of a scheme which aims to identify all deaths where drugs were involved[43]). Information on injecting is not recorded on the death certificate.**

In the early 1980s there appear to have been very few deaths associated with drug injecting in Glasgow[44]. An analysis of data from the Procurator Fiscal's office, the General Registrar Office and the Scottish HIV-test Register indicated that there were 51 deaths among drug injectors in Glasgow in 1989[45]. Given that there are about 300-350 deaths from all causes among people aged 15-35 per year in Glasgow, drug injecting was the most prevalent cause (directly or indirectly) of fatality among this age group. Unfortunately, since 1989 the trend has been upwards. Strathclyde police investigated 103/97 deaths in 1993/4 respectively among drug injectors.

If these figures represent a 1-2% mortality rate, then in 1989 there were 2,500-5,000 injectors increasing to 5,000-10,000 in 1994. As mentioned above, the 1-2% rate derives from drug injectors in treatment. If, as the CRM study indicates, only about 15% of Glasgow injectors were in-treatment at some point in 1990 and only 47% of a city-wide sample of injectors had ever received any form of treatment[46], then the mortality rate among out-of-treatment injectors may vary from the former group. The number of drug related deaths in Edinburgh and Glasgow also seems to be related to patterns of drug usage which, in turn, are related to availability of street and prescribed substances[47].

Clearly this method has limited applicability, although it can provide approximate estimates for heroin users and/or drug injectors. The sporadic and unpredictable occurrence of, for example, ecstasy related deaths, could not yield an estimate of ecstasy use (although some other indicator such as drug related emergencies might - see OPTION 4, SECTION 5).

Given the limitation of mortality data, one might conceivably use some other indicator such as the number of arrests for drugs offences. The problem with other indicators is that any multiplier is likely to be arbitrary, lacking the rationale of the mortality rate.


### 2.2.3. Network Analysis

Whereas CRM attempts to gauge the extent of the hidden population by statistical projection from two or more samples of known users, network analysis involves direct contact with small samples of users who provide information on their peers. The most comprehensive network analysis was conducted in the Wirral area of Merseyside in 1986 by Howard Parker and colleagues[17].

The Wirral has a population of about 340,000 which consists of 48 townships with populations ranging from 1,300 to 10,000. Four townships were chosen with varying levels of known heroin use. No townships with very low levels of known use were selected as these very 'invariably small villages in rural settings'.

In each of the four townships, a field-worker with extensive local knowledge and contacts, selected one known drug user as a respondent in the zero stage of the sampling process (see FIGURE 4). This process (of which there are many variants) involved 'snowballing' into drug networks by means of a referral chain, with each of the fifteen referrals being interviewed by the field-worker.

**FIGURE 4. Network analysis: sampling strategy used in four Wirral townships, 1985.**

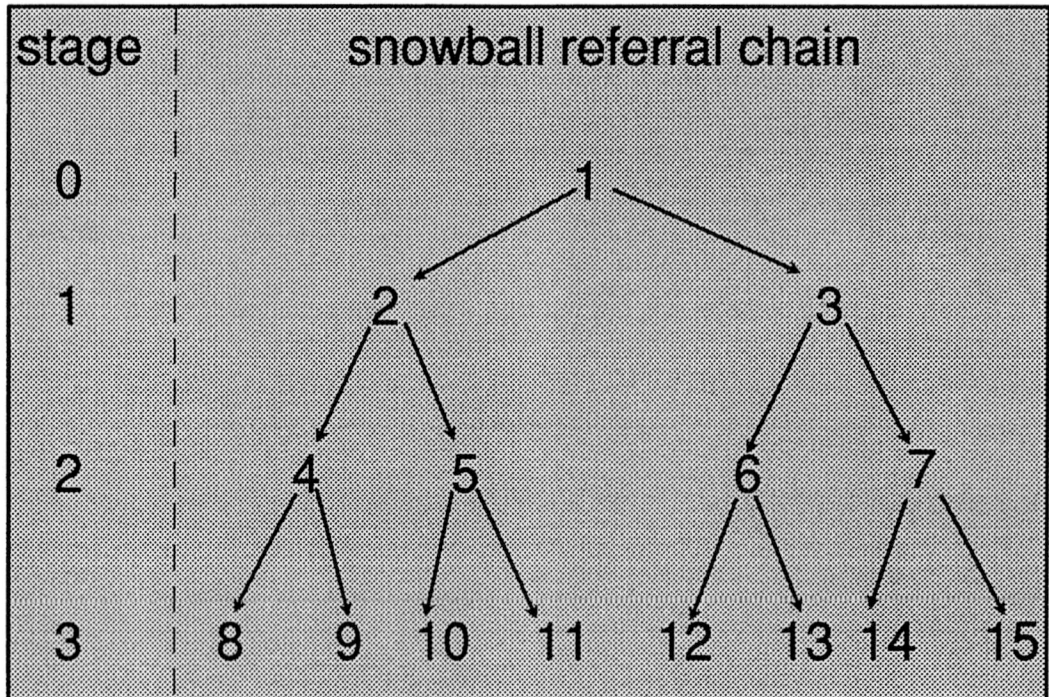

The success of network analysis depends on zero stage informants and there are a number of common sense steps which should be taken during their selection. They should be firmly established within a drug using network and should have good rapport with the field-worker. There are obvious dangers in using either peripheral or encyclopaedic informants whose referrals may produce biased data. Peripheral informants are likely to have minimal contact with other drug users while with encyclopaedic informants there is a danger that they have extensive contact with a sub-group of drug users. Unlike CRM, there has been little theoretical work to statistically underpin the validity of prevalence estimates resulting from network analysis[48].

Four methods were employed to estimate prevalence of opiate use in the Wirral.

*a. snowball ratio.*[*] The 60 referrals were asked if they had been in contact with (specified) agencies in the Wirral; their identifier information was then compared with known user lists from these agencies. The main problem with this method is that with only 15 cases in each township, the ratios of unknown:known are very sensitive to fluctuations in a small number of cases.

*b. nominee peer group.* The 60 referrals were then asked how many of their five closest friends (of the same sex and living in the same township) regularly used heroin during the previous year and, of these, how many had received treatment or been arrested for drugs offences during this period. Identifier information for

---

[*] Parker et al. refer to this as the snowball nominee method. The term snowball-ratio is used here to distinguish this method from the 'nominee peer group method' and the nominee-ratio method described below.

nominated peers was used to establish an unknown to known ratio for each township.

***c triangulation.*** The 60 referrals were asked to provide initials and gender for up to ten people who they knew to have taken heroin regularly in 1986. 7 people would not provide identifier information. The 53 remaining interviewees nominated 297 other persons. Removal of duplicates (same initials and gender) left 163 unique cases - of these 66 were identified as known users and 97 as hidden. The lack of identifier information may have eliminated persons who should have been included.

***d. snowball-recapture.*** Using the principles outlined above in SECTION 2.2.1, the population size was estimated using two-sample CRM. The first sample consisted of the 60 referrals produced by snowball method and the second of the 237 people 'known' to agencies in the four townships.

FIGURE 5. **Four methods used to estimate the ratio of unknown to known opiate users in the Wirral, 1985.**

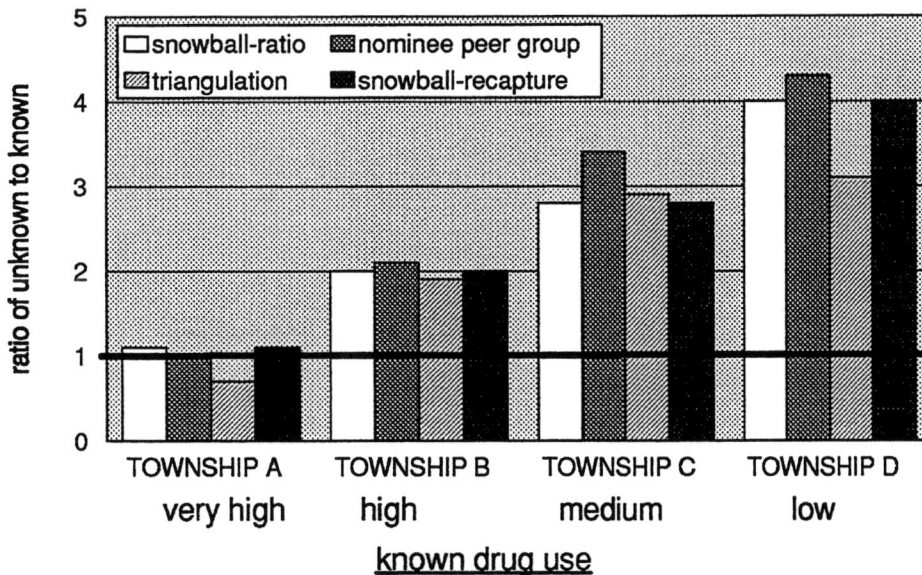

In comparing the four methods, FIGURE 5 shows that, except for township C, the triangulation ratios tend to be lower than those produced by the other three methods. All four methods, however, indicate that the ratio of unknown to known increases as the level of known drug use decreases. This is an important finding since it is goes against the common sense notion that unknown drug use is probably higher in areas of known use. (It also raises the question - what would have happened had the study been conducted in a fifth 'very low known prevalence' township?)

The application of four methods which produce fairly similar unknown to known ratios within townships suggests that each of the methods used are valid. However, it must be stressed that both methods and results cannot be separated from the context and there is **no guarantee that the same pattern of findings would be found in other locations**.

One drawback of nomination techniques is the requirement for supplying identifier information for friends or acquaintances. There may be communities where people would not be willing to give such information. One option would be to ask people nomination type questions but not request identifier information.

Suppose 15 people in a referral chain of the type illustrated in FIGURE 4 were asked:

**a) How many people do you personally know who have used drugs in the last year?**
**b) Of these how many have been in treatment in area X in the last year?**
**c) Of these how many have been arrested for drugs offences in X in the last year?**

Unlike the snowball ratio method, the number of unique cases is unknown, although the accuracy of nominee-ratio depends not on absolute numbers but the proportions of the numerator (nominees in treatment) and the denominator (nominees out of treatment) which are unique (see TABLE 11). If the proportion does not affect them differentially the estimate of unknown users will be accurate. If, however, the proportion of unique cases in the numerator is, for example, lower than in the denominator, the number of unknown users will be underestimated.

**TABLE 11. Comparison of snowball ratio and nominee ratio methods.**

| snowball ratio method | N | nominee ratio method | N |
|---|---|---|---|
| chain referrals | 15 | nominated drug users | 60 |
| chain referrals in treatment | 5 | nominees reported to be in treatment | 20 |
| chain referrals out of treatment | 10 | nominees reported to be out of treatment | 40 |
| total known in treatment in area X | 70 | total known in treatment in area X | 70 |
| estimated not in treatment | 140 | estimated not in treatment | 140 |
| estimated total number of drug users | 210 | total number of drug users | 210 |

As with the other network techniques, the nominee ratio method is subject to uncontrollable sources of error and estimates depend on the plausibility of the assumptions.

### 2.2.4. Synthetic Estimation and Extrapolation

This method can be applied where there is no information on drug use from the 'target' population but there is information on an 'ancillary' variable such as the crime rate[49]. In other settings where there is information on both crime and drug use it is possible to infer the level as illustrated in FIGURE 6. This method is only plausible if the relationship between drug use and the ancillary variable is the same (i.e. linear) in all three settings. As there is no way of establishing whether this is the case, there will always be doubt surrounding synthetic estimates.

FIGURE 6. Synthetic estimation of drug use - linear and non-linear relationships between crime and drug use.

**Synthetic Estimation**

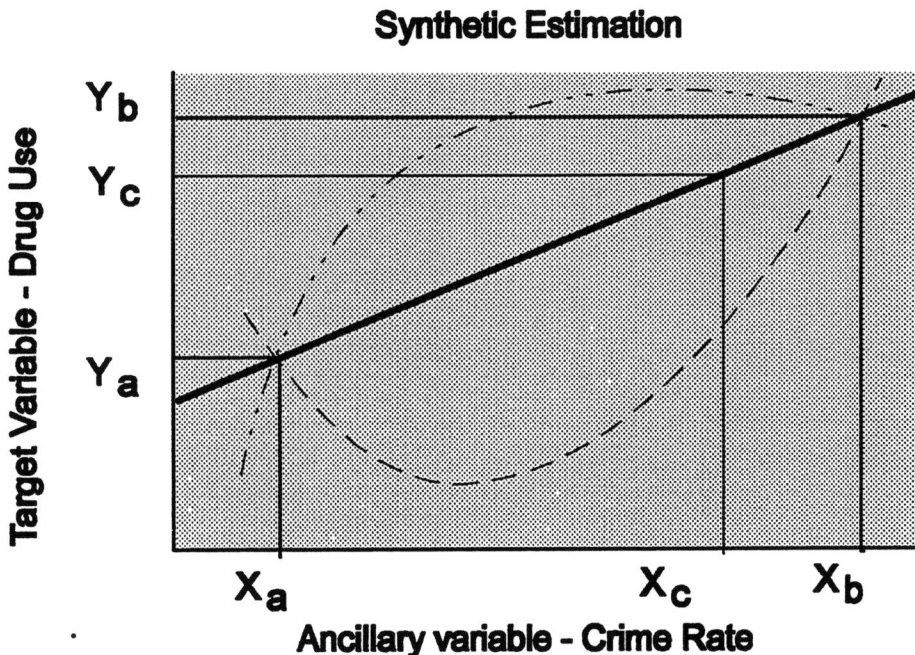

While there are at least two 'anchor' points in synthetic estimation, straightforward extrapolation relies on a single calibration point. For example, the estimate of 8,500 injectors in Glasgow 1990 can be extrapolated to the rest of Scotland simply by noting the population of other areas and assuming that there is a direct relationship between population and prevalence. This method, even more than synthetic estimation, depends on assumptions which are almost certainly invalid. The circumstances that gave rise to injecting in Glasgow are unlikely to have arisen elsewhere at the same time and in the same form.

## 2.3. OTHER METHODS

There are obvious difficulties in relying on self-reported information on drug use or recorded agency contacts. A radical alternative is to randomly test hair or urine specimens from the population of interest[50]. A recent study among 1,200 employees of a steel manufacturing plant in the United States noted that combined urine/hair analyses showed prevalence rates approximately 50% higher than self-report[51]. Dr Ian Oliver, Chief Constable of Grampian police, is an advocate of random drug testing in the work place in Scotland[52] - a proposal which has been strongly criticised as an infringement of civil liberties[53].

Hair analysis provides long-term information concerning the severity and pattern of drug use. In contrast urinalysis indicates drug use in the previous 2-3 days. Field studies suggest that hair analysis is considerably more effective at identifying drug users[54]. This is due to the wider surveillance window of hair analysis and the susceptibility of urinalysis to evasive measures. Both methods have complications with regard to false negatives and positives.

Ideally, policy makers would like models which specify a broad range of indicators and facilitate estimation of changing conditions. In rare cases where extensive data and advanced statistical skills are available it is possible to construct a <u>system dynamic model</u> which consists of an 'interconnected set of algebraic and differential equations representing the continuous ebb and flow of people, materials and information'[55]. It seems unlikely that sufficient information will be available to apply this method in Scotland in the foreseeable future.

# 3. SELECTING AN APPROPRIATE METHOD

It would not be prudent to give guidance on selecting an appropriate prevalence estimation method in an abstract context. As noted in SECTION 1.3 - it is essential to identify the appropriate types of epidemiological information for different policy objectives and the resources required for conducting investigations and analysis. This point was reinforced by considering three examples: local resource allocation to drug treatment programs, determining the extent of new recruitment into experimentation with drugs at a national level and the role of medical emergency trend data in formulating drug prevention policies.

Guidance on method selection must be tailored to specific requirements and, furthermore it should be recognised that guidance cannot be basely solely on scientific criteria. In many cases resources will be the determining factor while in other cases a given level of resources would purchase (for example) either a CRM study (see SECTION 2.2.1), a network analysis (see SECTION 2.2.4), or a cut-down version of both. This situation may well arise in Scottish health boards who wish to gain some idea of drug prevalence in their area. However, it could also be argued that the same information could be collected by a regular *national* population survey (see SECTION 2.1.3).

The decision as to which is the most appropriate method or methods to use should be a joint decision between purchasers and providers. (In SECTION 5, options for local and national co-ordination of purchasers and providers are considered). At an all-Scotland level, abstract guidance would probably be of little value without consideration of resources. In view of the diverse reasons for conducting prevalence studies, it is not possible to construct a flow-chart whereby answering a series of questions would lead to a specific method. Instead TABLE 12 classifies resources required and the degree of appropriateness for the methods reviewed in SECTION 2.

Ideally, TABLE 12 should be read in conjunction with SECTION 2 as it inevitably suffers from reducing complex information to a simple three point scoring system and, as with every attempt to formulate a general principle, there are bound to be exceptions.

**TABLE 12. Guide to selecting an appropriate prevalence estimation technique.**

| | direct | | | | indirect | | | | | other | |
|---|---|---|---|---|---|---|---|---|---|---|---|
| | enumer-ation [k] | needs assess-ment [k?] | population survey | local survey | capture-recapture | multiplier | network analysis | synthetic estimat-ion | extrap-olation | hair/urine analysis | system dynamic |
| 1 resources | * | ** | *** | ** | ** | * | ** | * | * | *** | ** |
| 2 statistical | * | * | ** | ** | *** | * | * | * | * | * | *** |
| 3 fieldwork | ** | ** | * | * | ** | * | ** | * | * | * | ** |
| 4 local | ** | *** | * | ** | ** | ** | *** | ** | * | *** | ** |
| 5 national | * | * | *** | * | * | ** | * | ** | * | * | ** |
| 6 urban | ** | ** | *** | ** | *** | ** | ** | ** | * | ** | *** |
| 7 rural | ** | ** | *** | *** | ** | * | *** | * | * | ** | * |
| 8 recreational drug use | * | ** | *** | *** | * | * | ** | ** | * | ** | ** |
| 9 problematic drug use | ** | ** | * | * | *** | ** | ** | ** | * | ** | ** |

key

| 1-3: | *=low | **=medium | ***=high | |
|---|---|---|---|---|
| 4-9: | *=not appropriate | **=sometimes appropriate | ***=usually appropriate | ****=usually appropriate |
| | | | | k=known drug use |

# 4. EVALUATION OF CURRENT SITUATION IN SCOTLAND

Prevalence estimation has increasingly come to be regarded as important for informing and evaluating a wide range of policies. For present purposes, discussion is restricted to available information on drug use in Scotland and the extent to which this information can be construed, either in its own right or when subjected to analysis, as prevalence estimates.

Before doing so, it may be useful to consider the views of Drug Action Team Chairpersons and Drug Misuse Co-ordinators in the 15 Scottish Health Board areas. SECTION 4.1 contains a digest of selected responses to a short questionnaire sent to them as part of the present review (see the APPENDIX).

## 4.1. VIEWS ON PREVALENCE ESTIMATION FROM SCOTTISH HEALTH BOARDS

While there were no prevalence estimates from the **Borders** a wide range of data (TABLE 13) have been found to be useful in planning and providing services between 1990-95.

**TABLE 13. Information on drug misuse, Borders Health Board, June 1995.**

1. Dingleton Hospital, a) use of in-patient beds for drug misuse, b) activity of Drug and Alcohol Resource Team (DART).
2. Borders General Hospital Trust in-patient data.
3. Registrar General-drug related deaths.
4. Drug Misuse Database, a) injecting practices, b) age of new drug misusers, c) comparison of proportion of new drug users aged 15-19 by health board, d) main problem drugs.
5. Needle exchange data, a) DART team, b) Boots pharmacies in Galashiels and Hawick, c) General Practitioners.
6. Prescribing trends from medical prescribing adviser, a) methadone b) temazepam.
7. 1993 Scottish Crime Survey.
8. 1993 Borders Drug Survey.
9. Anecdotal data in Addictions Forum.
10. Infectious disease information on HIV/Hepatitis B/Hepatitis C.

While these sources of information have been useful in planning/providing services, they also suggest an escalating drug problem in the Borders where, even now, demand for services is outstripping supply. The view was also expressed that existing surveillance/research was inadequate and that there should be a regular national survey in Scotland.

A contrasting view was expressed from **Forth Valley** where it was felt that too much reliance is placed on prevalence estimates, particularly with regard to the planning or utilisation of services. However, it was also felt that information on drug misuse has 'enabled service specifications to be developed and alterations to be made in the extent and range of services provided'. As in the Borders it was felt that existing surveillance/research is inadequate and that there should be a national survey.

In the **Highlands,** no estimates were reported for the number of drug users but there was a perception that drug misuse had increased between 1990-1995 and would continue to do so. Increased use was particularly evident for cannabis, amphetamine, LSD and tranquillisers. Various studies conducted in the region:

> *have generated a picture of patterns and trends in drug use in areas of the Highlands and the needs of drug users. This information has sometimes been met with denial and claims of exaggeration and has not necessarily aided service development in the short term.*

The view from this area was that although prevalence studies can be useful, caution needs to be exercised because of the methodological limitations, etc.

**Tayside** had fairly precise prevalence estimates (e.g. 8,000 volatile substance users aged less than 16) from two surveys but did not comment on whether the estimates were useful. There was scepticism regarding a national survey because of problems in deriving local estimates.

In **Lothian,** prevalence estimates were based on a wide variety of sources, ranging from surveys, fieldwork and projections (in the case of opioids diverted from prescription to non-prescription use). While drug misuse in general was thought to have increased from 1990 to 1995, heroin use was thought to have decreased and use of methadone and other opioids were stable. The main increase has been in ecstasy use (interestingly, the only drug reported to have declined in use in Tayside because it was 'too pricey and too dirty'). A wide range of data were available for 1990-95. HIV related data were used to plan/provide services. Data on problem drug use (surveys, fieldwork, seizures, arrests, information on market conditions) were used to inform educational activities and, where relevant, service providers.

Overall prevalence information is viewed as being useful but it is noted that studies should also try to obtain incidence data. Prevalence data on experimental and recreational use would also be useful. The view from Lothian is that prevalence data are 'moderately important' but services should be adaptable to deal with what comes through the door. Information on drug use has helped to justify requests for resources. While it was felt that a national survey should be conducted, this should be in conjunction with local surveys. Another function of surveys could be to help alter public attitudes to experimental drug use and the value of treatment and harm reduction services.

In **Shetland** a survey among young people conducted by the Shetland Council on Drugs and Alcohol indicated substantial levels of drug use among young people, particularly cannabis, ecstasy, mushrooms and volatile substances. Drug use is thought to have increased from 1990-95 and is forecast to further increase during the next five years. Prevalence and needs assessment studies are felt to be important as long as the local context is included. Overall, existing surveillance/research in Shetland was felt to be adequate, although there is scope for a national survey.

**TABLE 14. Summary of views and information on drug prevalence estimation in Scottish Health Board areas.**

1: There is no hard line dividing *information about* and *prevalence of* drug use in Scotland.

2: Despite the level of routine data and range of studies there is general dissatisfaction with existing surveillance/research.

3: Where reliable information is perceived to be available it is used in planning and providing services.

4: There is a widely held view that drug misuse will continue to increase over the next five years

5: There is considerable variation in planned activities relating to drug information.

6: There is a widely held view that a national survey of drug use would be useful, although not at the expense of local information.

7: Nearly all the data mentioned derive from the *direct* methods. The only exception is the CRM used in Glasgow to estimate prevalence of injecting. CRM is currently being used to estimate the prevalence of drug injecting in Edinburgh and Dundee.

# 5. CONCLUSIONS AND OPTIONS FOR FUTURE RESEARCH

The widespread belief that drug use will continue to increase over the next five years will, if true (and perhaps even if not true), have resource implications for various agencies. Yet it is clear that perceptions of the level of drug use in Scotland are largely based on interpretations, rather than analyses, of heterogeneous data. Paradoxically there is a vast amount of information concerning drug use but almost no prevalence data that meet internationally accepted scientific criteria.

Over the years there have been several reports calling for improved information on drug misuse in Scotland and there are current proposals for improving the quality of drug information throughout Europe. Rather than make recommendations, which in this field are easy to make but difficult to implement, a number of strategic options are outlined.

**Option 1. National Population Survey.** This would provide a focus for baseline prevalence estimation. In addition, a specialised drugs survey can provide detailed information on knowledge of and attitudes towards drugs. With sufficient sample size (at least 5,000 for Scotland) regional comparisons can be made. Provided the study methodology is kept constant, time trend analyses - particularly useful for monitoring the impact of educational and prevention policies - would also be possible. The cost of a regular national survey would, however, be substantial.

**Option 2. Co-ordinate Local Information Gathering.** At any one time there are likely to be a variety of mechanisms for collecting information on drug use in the Scottish regions. A co-ordinated approach, perhaps via the Scottish Advisory Committee on Drug Misuse and local Drug Action Teams, would aim to achieve comparability without enforcing uniformity (see also OPTION 5).

**Option 3: Enhance Data Collection.** Scotland has many excellent sources of data on drug use and users. There is one type of data which is increasingly being seen as an important epidemiological marker which is not collected in Scotland, namely drug related medical emergencies. An example of how such information can be obtained is provided by the Drug Abuse Warning Network (DAWN) in the United States[56]. This system established in 1972 consists of co-operating groups of reporting sources involved in 'servicing drug abusers who have become ill or died'. Reporting sources include hospital emergency rooms, crisis centers, coroners etc. One of the major advantages of DAWN is that it is able to report changes in drug use very soon after they occur. Overall the system 'provides a valuable window on the world of drug misuse' which is perhaps missing in Scotland. In Germany, for example, it is estimated that 5%-15% of drug addicts a year are medically treated as a result of a life threatening emergency situation[2]. A major impediment to establishing a medical emergency reporting scheme is the cost in terms of resources and manpower.

As recommended in the <u>Scottish Drugs Task Force Report</u>, social workers who come into contact with drug misusers should make returns to the Scottish Drug Misuse Database on form SMR23.

In relation to non-treatment agencies, an important contribution could be made by Scottish police forces (although there are considerable resource and ethical implications). In Germany, all police stations register those suspected of drug offences and those who show signs or state that they are taking hard drugs (heroin, cocaine, amphetamines, LSD). There are a number of methodological problems, e.g. police documentation does not provide information on duration of use (eg first time users vs long term addicts), data is retained for 2-10 years depending on the type of offence and there are regional variations in the way police forces record data. Despite these limitations, police data are central to prevalence estimation in Germany. Police data were also invaluable in estimating the prevalence of injecting in Glasgow (see SECTION 2.2.1).

**Option 4: Estimate Drug Injecting using Capture Recapture Methodology**: In urban areas where drug injecting is thought to occur, there should be regular capture-recapture studies. As discussed in SECTION 2.2.1, this method appears to provide the best way of estimating the prevalence of this form of drug use. Ideally, the studies (or surveillance) would be on-going, on the general principle that the more information there is, the more accurate the estimates will be.

**Option 5: Improve National Co-ordination.** At present there is no agency with a remit to a) collate the wide range of information which is potentially available across Scotland, b) analyse/interpret indicators and c) produce regular reports. While It is unlikely that a single organisation could easily be established it is possible to achieve most of the advantages of such an organization by linking the key existing organizations with accepted Scotland wide remits in the field. Such an initiative would build on existing skills, experience and knowledge of personnel within the individual organizations whilst encouraging optimum use of scarce resources and the avoidance of duplication of effort. The Scottish Centre for Infection and Environmental Health, the Information & Statistics and National Services Divisions of the Common Services Agency and the Scottish Drugs Forum have formulated a proposal to establish a new agency to be called the *Scottish Initiative for Drug Use Monitoring* [SIDUM]. SIDUM's main objectives are outlined in TABLE 15.

**TABLE 15. Main objectives for the proposed Scottish Initiative for Drug Use Monitoring [SIDUM].**

> 1. To provide a comprehensive and authoritative information and data analysis service relating to drug use in Scotland.
> 2. To work with similar agencies currently being established at the Institute for Drug Dependence (ISDD) in London and the European Monitoring Centre for Drugs and Drug Addiction (EMCDDA) in Lisbon.

The widespread belief that drug misuse will increase throughout Scotland in the next few years provides a challenge to those involved in education, prevention, treatment and law enforcement. It affords an opportunity to re-assess how best to measure the diverse forms of drug misuse in Scotland. It is also important to be realistic about what prevalence estimation can deliver. The introduction noted that prevalence estimation in the USA is only tangentially related to policy. While implementation of the options outlined above would improve prevalence estimation but would not produce definitive answers - for the simple reason that there are no definitive answers. Scotland could learn from the German experience, whereby prevalence estimation involves the accumulation and analysis of all available data in the country and the production of an authoritative range of estimates for various forms of drug misuse.

# 6. GLOSSARY

**CAPTURE-RECAPTURE (OR CONTACT-RECONTACT) METHOD** A method for estimating population size which involves three stages: 1) selecting samples of the population in question, 2) identifying overlapping cases, 3) using information about the relative degree of overlap to estimate the number of cases not observed in any of the samples.

**CASE** Person in the population or study group identified as having a particular disease, health disorder or condition under investigation. A variety of criteria may be used to identify cases, e.g. individual physicians' diagnoses, registries and notification, abstracts of clinical records, surveys of the general population and population screening. The epidemiologic definition of a case is not necessarily the same as the ordinary clinical definition[57].

**INCIDENCE RATE** The rate at which new events occur in a population. The numerator is the number of new events that occur in a defined period; the denominator is the population at risk of experiencing the event during the period[57].

**PREVALENCE RATE** The total number of instances of a given disease or other conditions in a given population at a designated time divided by the population at risk at this point in time. When used without qualification, the term usually refers to the situation at a specified point in time (point prevalence). Annual prevalence refers to the total number of persons with the disease or attribute at any time during a year. It includes cases of the disease or attribute arising before but extending into or through the year as well as those having their inception during the year[57].

**QUOTA SAMPLING** A method by which the proportions in the sample in various subgroups (according to criteria such as age, sex and socio-economic status of the individuals to be selected) are chosen to agree with the corresponding proportions in the population. The resulting sample may not be representative of characteristics that have not been taken into account[57].

# 7. REFERENCES

1       Lee RW. Dynamics of the Soviet illicit drug market. *Crime, Law and Social Change* 1992: 17 (3), 177-233.

2       Institut fur Therapieforschung. *Report on the methods of estimating the extent of the drug problems in Germany.* IFT: Munich, 1994.

3       Rutter M, Smith D. *Psychosocial disorders in young people.* Academia Europaea: London, 1995.

4       Scottish Office. *Drugs in Scotland: meeting the challenge. Report of ministerial drugs task force.* Scottish Office Home and Health Department: Edinburgh, 1994.

5       House of Commons Scottish Affairs Committee. *Drug Abuse in Scotland.* HMSO: London, 1994.

6       Rice D, Kelman S, Miller L. Economic cost of drug abuse. In Cartwright W & Kaple J. *Economic costs, cost-effectiveness, financing and community-based drug treatment.* National Institute on Drug Abuse; Research Monograph Series 113.

7       Sutton M, Maynard M. *What is the size and nature of the 'drug' problem in the UK?* Centre for Health Economics: York, 1992.

8       US Department of Health and Human Services. *Drug abuse and drug abuse research.* National Institute on Drug Abuse, Maryland, 1991.

9       Reuter P. Prevalence estimation and policy formulation. *Journal of Drug Issues* 1993: 23 (2), 167-184.

10      Hartnoll R. Epidemiological approaches to drug misuse in Britain *Journal of Addictive Diseases* 1991: 11 (1); 47-60.

11      Advisory Council on the Misuse of Drugs. *AIDS and drug misuse update.* HMSO: London, 1993.

12      Ashton M (editor). *National audit of drug misuse in the UK.* Institute for the Study of Drug Dependence: London: 1993.

13      San Miguel MT, Vila MN, Azorin MD, Sanz JA, Diaz MS, Bernal JM, Plaza J, Vazquez J, De La Rubia A.   Emergency room attentions due to adverse reactions to drugs (in Spanish). *Farmacia Clinica* 1992: 9 (8), 672-677.

14      Hartnoll R, Daviaud E, Lewis R, Mitcheson M. *Drug problems: assessing local needs. A practical manual for assessing the nature and extent of problematic drug use in a community.* Drug Indicators Project: London, 1985.

15      Hser Y, Anglin MD (editors). Prevalence estimation techniques for drug using populations. *Journal of Drug Issues* 23: 2, 163-360.

16      Information and Statistics Division of the Common Services Agency for The National Health Service in Scotland. *Scottish Drug Misuse Database Bulletin 1994.* ISD Publications: Edinburgh, 1994.

17      Parker H, Bakx K, Newcombe R. *Living with heroin.* Open University Press: Milton Keynes, 1988.

18      Daniel P. Problem drug use reported by services in Greater London. In M Ashton (editor) *National audit of drug misuse in the UK.* Institute for the Study of Drug Dependence: London, 1993.

19      Donmall M, Millar T. North West trends in presenting problem drug use, 1990-1992. In M Ashton (editor) *National audit of drug misuse in the UK.* Institute for the Study of Drug Dependence: London, 1993.

20      McKenna C. *Problem drug use and related needs in East Lothian.* Scottish Drugs Forum: Glasgow 1993.

21      Turner CF, Lessler JT, Gfroerer JC (editors). *Survey Measurement of drug use: methodological studies.* US Department of Health and Human Studies: Maryland, 1992.

22      Leitner M, Shapland J, Wiles P. *Drug usage and drug prevention: the views and habits of the general public.* HMSO: London, 1993.

23      Hammersley R. *Use of controlled drugs in Scotland: Findings from the 1993 Scottish Crime Survey.* Scottish Office Central Research Unit: Edinburgh, 1994

24      Coggans N, Shewan D, Henderson M & Davies JB. *National evaluation of drug education in Scotland.* Institute for the Study of Drug Dependence: London, 1991.

25      Hartnoll R. *Drug misuse trends in thirteen European cities.* Council of Europe Press: Strasbourg, 1994.

26      Begon M. *Investigating animal abundance: capture-recapture for biologists.* Edward Arnold, London, 1979.

27      Laporte R. Assessing the human condition: capture-recapture techniques. *British Medical Journal* 1994: 308; 5-6.

28      Bishop Y, Fienberg S, Holland P. *Discrete multivariate analysis: theory and practice.* MIT Press: Cambridge, 1975.

29      Pollock KH. Modeling capture, recapture and removal statistics for estimation of demographic parameters for fish and wildlife populations: past, present and future. *Journal of the American Statistical Association* 1991: 86, 413, 225-238.

30      Woodward JA, Retka R, Ng L. Construct validity of heroin abuse estimators. *The International Journal of the Addictions* 1984: 19 (1), 93-117.

31      McKeganey N, Barnard M, Watson H. HIV related risk behaviour among a non clinic sample of injecting drug users. *British Journal of Addiction* 1989: 8, 1481-1490.

32      Goldberg D, Watson H, Miller M. Pharmacy supply of needles and syringes - the effect on spread of HIV in intravenous drug misusers. Abstract 8521, *IV International Conference on AIDS.* Stockholm, July 1988.

33      Rahman MZ, Ditton J, Forsyth JM. Variations in needle sharing practices among intravenous drug users in Possil (Glasgow). *British Journal of Addiction* 1988: 84, 923-927.

34      Robertson JR, Bucknall AB, Welsby PD. Epidemic of AIDS related virus (HTLV/II/LAV) infection among intravenous drug users. British Medical Journal 1986: 292, 527-530.

35    Wald N, Law M, Meade T, Miller G, Alberman E, Dickson J. Use of personal medical records for research purposes. *British Medical Journal* 1994: 309, 1422-1424.

36    Frischer M, Leyland A, Cormack R, Goldberg D, Bloor M, Green S, Taylor A, Covell R, McKeganey N, Platt S. Estimating population prevalence of injection drug use and HIV infection among injection drug users in Glasgow. *American Journal of Epidemiology* 1993: 138 (3), 170-181.

37    Cormack RM. Log-linear models for capture-recapture. *Biometrics* 1989: 45: 395-413.

38    Cormack RM. Interval estimation for mark-recapature studies of closed populations. *Biometrics* 1992: 48, 567-576.

39    Payne CD. The GLIM (Generalized Linear Model) System-Release 3.77. Oxford: Numerical Algorithms, 1986.

40    Scottish Centre for Infection and Environmental Health. *Personal communication from the HIV & AIDS section.*

41    Oppenheimer E, Tobutt C, Taylor C, Andrew T. Death and survival in a cohort of heroin addicts from London clinics: a 22-year follow-up study. *Addiction* 1994: 89, 1299-1308.

42    Frischer M, Green S, Goldberg D. *Substance abuse related mortality: a world-wide review.* United Nations International Drug Control Program: Vienna, 1994.

43    Arrundale J, Cole SK. *Collection of information on drug related deaths by the General Register Office for Scotland.* GRO: Edinburgh 1995.

44    Haw S. *Drug problems in Greater Glasgow.* Standing Committee On Drug Abuse: Glasgow, 1985.

45    Frischer M, Bloor M, Goldberg D, Clark J, Green S, McKeganey N. Mortality among injecting drug users: a critical reappraisal. *Journal of Epidemiology and Community Health* 1993: 47, 59-63.

46    Rhodes T, Bloor M, Donoghoe M, Haw S, Ettore E, Platt S, Frischer M, Hunter G, Taylor A, Finlay A, Crosier A, Stephens S, Covell R, Stimson G, Goldberg D, Green S, McKeganey N. HIV prevalence and HIV risk behaviour among injecting drug users in London and Glasgow. *AIDS Care* 1993: 5; 413-426.

47    Hammersley R, Cassidy M, Oliver J. Drugs associated with drug related deaths in Edinburgh and Glasgow, November 1990 to October 1992. *Addiction* 1995: 90, 959-965.

48    Biernacki P, Waldorf D. Snowball sampling: problems and techniques of chain referral sampling. *Sociological Methods and Research* 1981: 10, 141-161.

49    Wickens TD. Quantitative methods for estimating the size of a drug-using population. *Journal of Drug Issues* 1993: 23(2), 185-216.

50    Strang J, Black J, Marsh A, Smith B. Hair analysis for drugs: technological breakthrough or ethical quagmire? *Addiction* 1993: 88 (2), 163-166.

51    Cook RF, Bernstein AD, Arrington TL, Andrews CM, Marshall GA. Methods for assessing drug use prevalence in the workplace: a comparison of self-report, urinanalysis and hair analysis. *International Journal of the Addictions* 1995: 30 (4), 403-426.

52    Arlidge J, Bennetto J. Police chief says firms should test for drugs. London: *Independent* 29th September 1995.

53    Sharkey A. Dear Ian Oliver. London: *Independent* 30th August 1995.

**54**    DuPont RL, Baumgartner WA. Drug testing by urine and hair analysis: complementary features and scientific issues. *Forensic Science International* 1995 70, 63-76

**55**    Homer JB. A system dynamics model for cocaine prevalence estimation and trend projection. *Journal of Drug Issues* 1993: 23 (2), 251-279.

**56**    Winick C. Epidemiology of alcohol and drug abuse. In *Substance abuse: a comprehensive textbook (second edition)* edited by JH Lowinson P Ruiz RB Millman JG Langrod. Williams & Wilkins: Baltimore, 1992.

**57**    Last JM. A Dictionary of epidemiology (second edition). Oxford University Press: Oxford, 1988.

# 8. APPENDIX: QUESTIONNAIRE SENT TO DRUG MISUSE CO-ORDINATORS AND CHAIRPERSONS OF DRUG ACTION TEAMS

## PREVALENCE OF DRUG MISUSE IN SCOTTISH HEALTH BOARD AREAS

*\* Please attach separate sheets or photocopies of this sheet if required.*

**1.** What is your best estimate of the *number* of current drug users -in each of the categories below - in your health board area (HBA) [Codes may be used in tables 1B,2 & 3].

| AGE GROUP | VOLATILE SUBSTANCES | CANNABIS | ECSTASY | HEROIN | WITHOUT/IN EXCESS OF PRESCRIPTION [SPECIFY] | OTHER DRUGS [SPECIFY] |
|---|---|---|---|---|---|---|
| up to 16 | [A1]: | [B1]: | [C1]: | [D1]: | [E1]: | [F1]: |
| 16-44 | [A2]: | [B2]: | [C2]: | [D2]: | [E2]: | [F2]: |
| 45 and over | [A3]: | [B3]: | [C3]: | [D3]: | [E3]: | [F3]: |

**1B.** Source of information for any estimates given. Please tick appropriate category.

| AGE GROUP/DRUG TYPE | BEST GUESS | "DATA" [SPECIFY] | SURVEY/RESEARCH [SPECIFY] |
|---|---|---|---|
|  |  |  |  |
|  |  |  |  |
|  |  |  |  |
|  |  |  |  |

**2. What is your perception of changes in drug use in your HBA in the *previous* five years?**

|  | DECLINING | STABLE | INCREASING |
|---|---|---|---|
| DRUG MISUSE [IN GENERAL] |  |  |  |
| SPECIFIC SUBSTANCE [_____] |  |  |  |
| SPECIFIC SUBSTANCE [_____] |  |  |  |
| SPECIFIC SUBSTANCE [_____] |  |  |  |
| SPECIFIC SUBSTANCE [_____] |  |  |  |

**3. How do you think drug misuse will change in your health board area (HBA) over the *next* five years?**

|  | DECLINE | STABLE | INCREASE |
|---|---|---|---|
| DRUG MISUSE [IN GENERAL] |  |  |  |
| SPECIFIC SUBSTANCE [_____] |  |  |  |
| SPECIFIC SUBSTANCE [_____] |  |  |  |
| SPECIFIC SUBSTANCE [_____] |  |  |  |
| SPECIFIC SUBSTANCE [_____] |  |  |  |

**4. Briefly describe sources of information on the extent of drug misuse in your HBA between 1990 and 1995.**

_____

_____

**5. Do you think that prevalence estimates are an important for planning and/or providing services to drug users?**

YES/NO. _If yes, briefly specify what you think the most relevant data would be. If no, why not._

_____

_____

**6. Overall, has information on the scale of drug misuse been useful in planning or providing services to drug users in your HBA from 1990 to 1995?**

YES/NO. _If yes, briefly specify which data and how._

_____

_____

**7. Can you briefly describe any plans for determining the nature and extent of drug misuse in your HBA from 1996 onwards?**

_____

_____

**8. Do you think existing surveillance/research provides sufficient information on drug use:**

a) in your HBA: YES/NO        b) in Scotland: YES/NO

**9. Do you think that there should be a regular national survey of drug use/misuse in Scotland.**

YES/NO.

**10. Any other comments?**

_____

_____

# CRU RESEARCH - RECENTLY PUBLISHED WORK

**The Measurement of Changes in Road Safety** : A Consultant's Report by the Ross Silcock Partnership. (1991) *(£5.00)*

**Socio-legal Research in the Scottish Courts - Volume 2** : Michael Adler and Ann Millar. (1991) *(£4.00)*

**Crime Prevention in Scotland - Findings from the 1988 British Crime Survey** : David M Allen and Douglas Payne. (1991) *(£4.00)*

**The Public and the Police in Scotland - Findings from the 1988 British Crime Survey** : David M Allen and Douglas Payne. (1991) *(£4.00)*

**Ethnic Minorities in Scotland** : Patten Smith (Social and Community Planning Research). (1991) *(£8.50)*

**Adoption and Fostering - The Outcome of Permanent Family Placements in Two Scottish Local Authorities.** (1991) *(£5.50)*

**Adoption Services in Scotland - A Summary** : **Recent Research Findings and their Implications:** John Triseliotis (Edinburgh University). (1991) *(£4.00)*

**Children with Epilepsy and their Families - Needs and Services** : A Laybourn and M Hill (Glasgow University). (1991) *(£4.00)*

**Community Ownership in Glasgow - An Evaluation** : David Clapham, Keith Kintrea and Leslie Whitefield (Centre for Housing Research, Glasgow University), Frances Macmillan and Norman Raitt (Norman Rait Architects, Edinburgh). (1991) *(£12.50)*

**Small Claims in the Sheriff Court in Scotland - An Assessment of the Use and Operation of Procedure** : Helen Jones, Alison Platts, Jacqueline Tombs (CRU); Cowan Irvine, James McManus (University of Dundee); Kenneth Miller, Alan Paterson (University of Strathclyde). (1991) *(£5.00)*

**Physical Evaluation of Community Ownership Schemes** : Frances Macmillan and Norman Raitt (Norman Raitt Architects, Edinburgh). (1991) *(£10.00)*

**The Impact of Environmental Design Upon the Incidence and Type of Crime - A Literature Review** : Jonathan Bannister (Centre for Housing Research, Glasgow University). (1991) *(£5.00)*

**Preventing Vehicle Theft - A Policy-Oriented View of the Literature** : Ronald V Clarke (State University of New Jersey). (1991) *(£4.00)*

**The Location of Alcohol Use by Young People - A Review of the Literature** : Neil Hutton (School of Law, Strathclyde University). (1991)

**Setting up Community Care Projects - A Practice Guide:** Anne Connor. (1991)

**Local Authority Housing Stock Transfers** : Tom Duncan

(The Planning Exchange, Glasgow). (1991) *(£4.50)*

**Competitive Tendering in Scotland - A Survey of Satisfaction with Local Authority Services** : A Consultant's Report by The MVA Consultancy. (1991) *(£4.00)*

**Public Attitudes to the Environment in Scotland** : Diana Wilkinson and Jennifer Waterton. (1991) *(£4.00)*

**Text Creation in the Scottish Office - The Experience, Expectations and Perceptions of the Users and Providers of Services: (A report on surveys of four groups of Scottish Office staff carried out by The Special Projects Branch of The Scottish Office Central Research Unit as part of an Efficiency Scrutiny of Text Creation in The Scottish Office):** Hugh Gentleman and Susan A Hughes. (1992)

**Where the Time Goes - The Allocation of Administration and Casework Between Client Groups in Scottish Departments of Social Work** : John Tibbit and Pauline Martin. (1992) *(£4.00)*

**Financial Management of Mentally Incapacitated Adults - Characteristics of Curatories** : Fiona Rutherdale. (1992) *(£4.00)*

**Evaluation of the Care and Repair Initiative in Scotland - Study Report** : PIEDA and Norman Rait Architects. (1992) *(£5.00)*

**Register of Research (1992-93 Edition)** : (1992)

**The Hidden Safety Net ? - Mental Health Guardianship: Achievements and Limitations** : Carole Moore, Anne Connor, Pauline Martin and John Tibbitt. (1992) *(£5.00)*

**Crime in Scotland - Findings from the 1988 British Crime Survey** : Douglas Payne. (1992) *(£4.00)*

**Crime and the Quality of Life - Public Perceptions and Experiences of Crime in Scotland: Findings from the 1988 British Crime Survey** : Richard Kinsey and Simon Anderson. (1992) *(£4.00)*

**The Deferred Sentence in Scotland** : Linda Nicolson. (1992) *(£5.00)*

**Social Work Department Reviews of Children in Care** : Andrew Kendrick and Elizabeth Mapstone. (1992) *(£10.00)*

**Retail Impact Assessment Methodologies** : Consultant's Report by Drivers Jonas, Glasgow. (1992) *(£6.00)*

**Section 50 Agreements** : Consultant's Report by Jeremy Rowan Robinson and Roger Durman. (1992) *(£6.00)*

**Evaluation of Scottish Road Safety Year 1990:** Jennifer Waterton. (1992) *(£5.00)*

**The Witness in the Scottish Criminal Justice System** : Anne Stafford and Stewart Asquith. (1992) *(£4.00)*

**Good Practice in Housing Management - A Literature Review** : Mary Taylor & Fiona Russell, Dept. of Applied Social Science, Dr Rob Ball , Dept. of Management Science, University of Stirling (in association with The Institute of Housing in Scotland). (1992) *(£4.00)*

**Sexual History and Sexual Character Evidence in Scottish Sexual Offence Trials - A Study of Scottish Court Practice under ss. 141A/141B and 346A/346B of the Criminal Procedure (Scotland) Act 1975 as inserted by the Law Reform (Miscellaneous Provisions)(Scotland) Act 1985 s. 36** : Beverley Brown, Michelle Burman and Lynn Jamieson. (1992) *(£4.50)*

**Neighbourhood Watch - A Literature Review** : Louise Brown. (1992) *(£4.00)*

**Strathclyde Police Red Light Initiative - Accident Monitor** : MVA Consultancy in association with Jennifer Waterton. (1992) *(£5.00)*

**The Rent to Mortgage Scheme in Scotland** : Helen Kay and Jeremy Hardin. (1992) *(£4.00)*

**Probation In Scotland - Policy and Practice** : Roslyn Ford, Jason Ditton and Ann Laybourn. (1992) *(£5.00)*

**The Probation Alternative - Case Studies in the Establishment of Alternative to Custody Schemes in Scotland**: Anne Creamer, Linda Hartley and Bryan Williams. (1992) *(£5.00)*

**The Probation Alternative - A Study Of The Impact of Four Enhanced Probation Schemes On Sentencing:** Anne Creamer, Linda Hartley and Bryan Williams. (1992) *(£5.00)*

**Evaluation of Compulsory Competitive Tendering for Local Authority Services** : Richard Evans. (1992) *(£4.00)*

**The Review of Residential Child Care in Scotland - The Three Supporting Research Studies** : Andrew Kendrick, Sandy Fraser, Moira Borland and Juliet Harvey. (1992) *(£5.00)*

**Education in and out of School - The Issues and the Practice in Inner Cities and Outer Estates** : John MacBeath. (1992) *(£5.50)*

**The Use of Judicial Separation** : Alison Platts. (1992) *(£4.00)*

**Policing in the City - Public, Police and Social Work** : Richard Kinsey. (1993) *(£4.50)*

**Counting Travellers in Scotland - The 1992 Picture** : Hugh Gentleman. (1993) *(£4.50)*

**Crime Prevention and Housebreaking in Scotland:** David McAllister, Susan Leitch and Douglas Payne. (1993) *(£4.00)*

**Supporting Victims of Serious Crime:** Rebbecca Dobash, Pat McLauglin and Russell Dobash. (1993) *(£4.00)*

**Prohibiting the Consumption of Alcohol in Designated Areas:** Janet Ruiz. (1993) *(£4.50)*

**Appeals in the Scottish Criminal Courts:** Ann Millar. (1993) *(£4.50)*

**The Attitudes of Young Women Drivers to Road Safety:** Cragg, Ross & Dawson Ltd. (1993) *(£5.00)*

**The Management of Child Abuse - A Longitudinal Study of Child Abuse in Glasgow:** Ann Laybourn and Juliet Harvey. (1993) *(£5.00)*

**Supporting Victims in the Criminal Justice System - A study of a Scottish sheriff Court:** Rosemary I Wilson. (1993) *(£4.00)*

**Consideration of the Mental State of Accused Persons at the Pre-Trial and Pre-Sentencing Stages:** G. D.L. Cameron, J. J. McManus. (1993) *(£4.00)*

**Process & Preference - Assessment of Older People for Institutional Care:** Elaine Samuel, Sue Brace, Graham Buckley and Susan Hunter. (1993) *(£5.50)*

**Untying the Knot: Characteristics of Divorce in Scotland:** Sue Morris, Sheila Gibson and Alison Platts. (1993) *(£5.00)*

**The Practice of Arbitration in Scotland 1986-1990:** Dr Fraser P Davidson. (1993) *(£5.00)*

**Police Specialist Units for the Investigation of Crimes of Violence Against Women and Children In Scotland:** Ms M Burman and Ms S Lloyd. (1993) *(£5.00)*

**Local Authority Housing Waiting Lists in Scotland:** Sarah Dyer. (1993) *(£4.50)*

**The Right to Buy in Scotland - An Assessment of the Impact of the First Decade of the Right to Buy:** Karen MacNee. (1993) *(£4.00)*

**A Better Start - Social Work Service Projects for Homeless Young People** (1993): Anne Conner and Debbie Headrick.
*Part 1: The Experience of The Scottish Office Rooflessness Report*
*Part 2: The Scottish Office Rooflessness Initiative - Background and Research Findings*

**The Effects of Privatisation of the Scottish Bus Group and Bus Deregulation:** Consultant's Report by The Transport Operations Research Group, Newcastle University. (1993) *(£3.00)*

**The Voluntary Sector and the Environment:** Alistair McCulloch, Seaton Baxter and John Moxen. (1993) *(£3.00)*

**Social Work Responses to the Misuse of Alcohol - A Literature Review:** Murray Simpson, Bryan Williams and Andrew Kendrick. (1993) *(£4.50)*

**Socio - legal Research in the Scottish Courts Vol 3** : (eds)Michael Adler, Ann Millar & Sue Morris (1993)*(£5.00)*

**Process and Preference - Assessment of Older People for Institutional Care:** Elaine Samuel, Sue Brace, Graham Buckley and Susan Hunter. (1993) *(£5.50)*

**Review of Retailing Trends:** John Dawson. (1994) *(£7.50)*

**Empty Public Sector Dwellings in Scotland - A Study of Empty Public Sector Housing in Scotland in 1992:** Alan Murie, Sally Wainwright and Keith Anderson, School of Planning and Housing, Edinburgh College of Art/ Heriot-Watt University. (1994) *(£5.50 )*

**An Evaluation of "Cars Kill" Television Commercial:** Research carried out on behalf of the Scottish Road Safety Campaign by System Three Scotland. (1994) *(£5.00)*

**The Code of Guidance on Homelessness in Scotland - Local Authority Policies and Practice:** Richard Evans, Nicholas Smith, Caroline Bryson and Nicola Austin. (1994) *(£6.50)*

**Operating Bail - Decision Making Under the Bail etc. (Scotland) Act 1980:** Fiona Paterson and Claire Whittaker. (1994) *(£15.95 from HMSO )*

**Literature Review of Rural Issues:** Karen MacNee. (1994) *(£5.00)*

**Review of Scottish Coastal Issues:** Consultant's Report by Peter R Burbridge and Veronica Burbridge. (1994) *(£5.00)*

**Detention and Voluntary Attendance of Suspects at Police Stations:** The MVA Consultancy. (1994) *(£5.00)*

**Police User Surveys in Scotland:** Dr Nicholas R Fyfe. (1994) *(£5.00)*

**Evaluation of The Scottish Road Safety Campaign's Initiatives in Relation to the Year of the Eldery :** Resarch carried out on behalf of the Scottish Road Safety Campaign by the MVA Consultancy. (1994) *(£5.00)*

**Criminal Justice and Related Services for Young Adult Offenders :** Stewart Asquith and Elaine Samuel. (1994) *(£11.95 from HMSO )*

**Neighbourhood Disputes in the Criminal Justice System** R. E. MacKay and S.R. Moody with Fiona Walker. (1994) *(£5.00)*

**Attitudes of Scottish Drivers Towards Speeding - 1994 Survey :** A Survey of Scottish Drivers conducted by Market Research Scotland Ltd on behalf of the Scottish Office. (1994) *(£5.00)*

**A Review Of the Use Classes Order :** Janet Brand (Strathclyde University) in association with David Bryce and Niall McClure (James Barr & Son, Chartered Surveyors). (1994) *(£5.00)*

**Review of Census Applications :** Pauline Martin. (1994) *(£5.00)*

**Monetary Penalties in Scotland :** Linda Nicholson. (1994) *(£13.95 from HMSO )*

**Multi-Party Actions In Scotland :** Dr. Christine Barker, Professor Ian D Willock and Dr. James J McManus. (1994) *(£5.00)*

**Diversion from Prosecution to Psychiatric Care:** Dr Peter Duff and Michelle Burman. (1994) *(£5.00)*

**Opening and Reopening Adoption - Views From Adoptive Families:** Linda Paterson (Abridged by Malcolm Hill). (1994) *(£5.00)*

**The Use of The Judicial Examination Procedure in Scotland:** Susan Leitch. (1994) *(£5.00)*

**A Fine on Time - The Monitoring and Evaluation of the Pilot Supervised Attendance Order Schemes:** Louise Brown. (1994) *(£4.00)*

**Use of Controlled Drugs in Scotland - Findings from the 1993 Scottish Crime Survey:** Richard Hammersley, Behavioural Sciences Group, University of Glasgow. (1994) *(£5.00)*

**Evaluation of the Safer Edinburgh Project:** James K Carnie. (1994) *(£5.00)*

**Dundee NE Safer Cities Project 1994 Household Survey Report:** H.R. Jones, D.E. Short and W.G. Berry, Department of Geography,The University,Dundee. (1994) *(£5.00)*

**Child Sexual Abusers:** Lorraine Waterhouse, Russell P Dobash and James Carnie. (1994) *(£6.00)*

**Case Finding for Care Management for Elderly People - A Study of Existing Information Sources:** Alex Robertson, Colin Currie and Eileen Brand. (1994) *(£5.00)*

**The Role of The Mental Health Officer :** Marion Ulas , Fiona Myers and Bill Whyte, Department of Social Policy and Social Work, Edinburgh University. (1994) *(£6.00)*

**An Evaluation of Community Involvement in The Whitfield Partnership :** Andrew McArthur, Annette Hastings and Alan McGregor, Training and Employment Research Unit, Glasgow University. (1994) *(£5.00)*

**An Evaluation of Community Involvement in The Ferguslie Park Partnership :** William Roe Associates. (1994) *(£5.00)*

**Living in Castlemilk :** Anne Corden and Mhairi Mackenzie with Claire Norris. (1994) *(£5.00)*

**Perceptions of Drug Control Problems and Policies -A Comparison of Scotland and Holland in the 1980's :** Sally Haw and Jason Ditton. (1995) *(£5.00)*

**What Works in Situational Crime Prevention ? A Literature Review :** Linda Nicholson. (1995) *(£5.00)*

**Deprived Areas in Scotland :** George Duguid. (1995) *(£5.00)*

**Live Television Link - An Evaluation of its Use by Child Witnesses in Scottish Criminal Trials :** Kathleen Murray. (1995) *(£7.00)*

**Sustainable Development - What it Means to the General Public :** Ewen McCaig and Charlie Henderson (The MVA Consultancy). (1995) *(£5.00)*

**Information Needs of Victims:** The MVA Consultancy. *(1995) (£5.00)*

**Implementation and Monitoring of the Children Act 1989 Part X and Section 19:** Maureen Buist. (1995) *(£5.00)*

**Social Work Placements in Scottish Local Authorities:** Fiona M Fraser. (1995) *(£5.00)*

**Running The Red - An Evaluation of The Strathclyde Police Red Light Camera Initiative:** The MVA Consultancy. (1995) *(£5.00)*

**Feuing Conditions in Scotland:** Professor D. J. Cusine and M's J. Egan. (1995) *(£5.00)*

**Review of Neighbour Notification:** School of Planning & Housing, Edinburgh College of Art/ Heriot Watt University and Peter PC Allan Ltd. (1995) *(£5.00)*

**Specialism in Private Legal Practice:** Dr Karen Kerner. (1995) *(£5.00)*

**Housing Management CCT in Rural Authorities:** Douglas Johnston and Andrew Thomson, CSL-Touche Ross Management Consultants. (1995) *(£5.00)*

**Management Options for Regional Parks - A Discussion Paper:** Peter Scott Planning Services in association with Rosalind Pearson. (1995) *(£5.00)*

**Accessing Enviromental Information in Scotland:** John Moxen and Alistair McCulloch with Dorothy Williams and Seaton Baxter. (1995) *(£5.00)*

**Enviromental Education -**
**Is The Message Getting Through ? :** Michele Corrado and Andrea Nove (MORI). (1995) *(£5.00)*

**Residential Care in the Intergration of Child Care Services:** Andrew Kendrick Dept. Of Social Work, University of Dundee. (1995) *(£5.00)*

**Baseline Study of Public Knowledge and Perceptions of Local Goverment in Scotland:** The MVA Consultancy. (1995) *(£5.00)*

**An Evaluation of Scotland's National Tourist Routes:** Colin Buchanan & Partners. (1995) *(£5.00)*

**Public Interest and Private Grief - A Study of Fatal Accident Inquiries in Scotland:** Simon Anderson, Susan Leitch and Sue Warner. (1995) *(£5.00)*

**Pilgrim's Process ? - Defended Actions In The Sheriff's Ordinary Court:** Sue Morris and Debbie Headrick. (1995) *(£5.00)*

**Register of Research** . (1995) *(£4.00)*

**The Cost and Quality of Care for People with Disabilities:** E. Brand, M. King, I. Lapsley and S. Llewellyn. (1995) *(£5.00)*

**Interim Evaluation of The Castlemilk Partnership:**

Mo O'Toole, Dawn Snape and Murray Stewart (School Advanced Urban Studies, University of Bristol).

(1995) *(£5.00)*

**Interim Evaluation of The Ferguslie Park Partnership:** Lucy Gaster, Gavin Smart, Lyn Harrison, Ray Forrest and Murray Stewart (School for Advanced Urban Studies, University of Bristol). (1995) *(£5.00)*

**Interim Evaluation of The Wester Hailes Partnership:** Alan McGregor, Keith Kintrea, Iain Fitzpatrick, and Alison Urquhart (Centre for Housing Research and Urban Studies University of Glasgow). (1995) *(£5.00)*

**Interim Evaluation of The Whitfield Partnership:** Keith Kintrea, Alan McGregor, Margaret McConnachie and Alison Urquhart (Centre for Housing Research and Urban Studies, University of Glasgow). (1995) *(£5.00)*

**Analysis of Urban Partnership Household Surveys (Castlemilk, Ferguslie Park, Westerhailes, Whitfield):** Charlie Henderson (The MVA Consultancy). (1995) *(£5.00)*

**An Evaluation of The Scottish Office Domestic Violence Media Campaign:** Susan MacAskill and Douglas Eadie (Centre for Social Marketing, University of Strathclyde) and System Three Scotland. (1995) *(£5.00)*

**Personal Injury Litigation in the Scottish Courts: A Descriptive Analysis:** Gordon Cameron with Robin Johnston, University of Dundee. (1995) *(£5.00)*

**Patterns of Custodial Sentencing in the Sheriff Court:** Neil Hutton and Cyrus Tata, School of Law, University of Strathclyde. (1995) *(£5.00)*

**Directory of Crime Prevention Initiatives in Scotland:** Compiled by Claire Valentin. (1995) *(free publication)*

**A Baseline Study of Housing Management in Scotland:** David Clapham, Keith Kintrea, John Malcolm, Hilary Parkey and Suzie Scott (Centre for Housing and Urban Studies). (1995) *(£10.00)*

**A Baseline Study of Housing Management in Scotland (Summary Report):** David Clapham, Keith Kintrea, John Malcolm, Hilary Parkey and Suzie Scott (Centre for Housing and Urban Studies). (1995) *(£3.00)*

**Evaluation of Land Cover of Scotland 1988:** Richard Dunn (Independent Consultant in GIS) in association with Carys Swanwick (Land Use Consultants) and Dr Andrew Harrison. (1995) *(£5.00)*

**Partnership in the Regeneration of Urban Scotland:** (HMSO) (1996)

**The Safer Cities Programme in Scotland - Evaluation of Safe Greater Easterhouse:** Dr James K Carnie. (1996) *(£5.00)*

**The Safer Cities Programme in Scotland - Evaluation of Dundee North East:** Dr James K Carnie. (1996) *(£5.00)*

**The Safer Cities Programme in Scotland - Evaluation of Safe Castlemilk:** Dr James K Carnie. (1996) *(£5.00)*

**The Safer Cities Programme in Scotland - Overview Report:** Dr James K Carnie. (1996) *(£5.00)*

**Does Closed Circuit Television Prevent Crime?:** Emma Short and Dr Jason Ditton, Scottish Centre for Criminology. (1996) *(£2.50)*

**Evaluation of Speedwatch:** System Three Scotland. (1996) (£5.00)

**Proactive Policing - An Evaluation of the Central Scotland Police Crime Management Model:** Peter Amey, Chris Hale and Steve Uglow, Canterbury Business School, University of Kent. (1996) (£5.00)

**The Pedestrian Casualty Problem in Scotland - Why So Many?:** Gordon Harland and Derek Halden, Transport Research Laboratory. (1996) *(£5.00)*

**Energy Conversation and Planning:** Howard Liddel, Drew Mackie and Gillian Macfarlane (GAIA Planning Consultants). (1996) *(£5.00)*

**The Speeding Driver:** Colin Buchanan & Partners. (1996) *(£5.00)*

**Foreign Language Interpreters in the Scottish Criminal Court:** The MVA Consultancy. (1996) *(£5.00)*

**Grounds of Appeal in Criminal Cases:** Dr Peter Duff and Frazer McCallum, Law Faculty, Aberdeen University. (1996) *(£7.00 from HMSO)*

**Assessment of the Implications of Radium Contamination of Dalgety Bay Beach and Foreshore:** Dr B Heaton, Professor F Glasser, Miss S Jones, Dr N Bonney, Mr A Glendinning and Dr D Sell (University of Aberdeen and Auris Enviromental Ltd). (1996) *(£10.00)*

**Scoping Study on Rural Development Issues in Scotland:** Pollyanna Chapman, Ed Conway and Mark Shucksmith (Arkleton Centre for Rural Development Research, Aberdeen University). (1996) *(£5.00)*